CU00820222

Matt Moran

when I get home

with photography by Alan Benson

LANTERN
an imprint of
PENGUIN BOOKS

contents

introduction

Believe it or not, most people think I don't cook at home. They think because I have a fine dining restaurant that by the time I get home the last thing I want to do is cook. The opposite is true. I love cooking at home. Food for the family. Food for friends. Food for the soul.

When I've got the day off, the first thing I think about in the morning is what I'm going to eat. I like to keep it simple and to work around what is in season. Good food at home can be so easy to do. Go down to your local grocer, butcher or growers' market. Today we are so blessed with our farmers' markets – there is always something new and exciting. It reminds me of the days when I was at Paddington Inn. To come up with dishes, I'd just walk into the local fruit market and see what was available. I urge you to do the same.

If I'm cooking for the family or having people over for a Sunday lunch, these are the recipes I use. When I entertain, the last thing I want to do is cook ARIA food. It needs to be simple and easy.

To me the heart of any home is the kitchen. I love an entertaining area that revolves around the kitchen, where the preparation and cooking can be done with friends standing and chatting around the kitchen bench. And being a chef I find it really important to show my kids what good food is all about and get them involved in it.

When asked to do this book I thought about what recipes to include, and for two years every time I cooked a meal at home I'd write it down. These are the recipes I love. These are the recipes that don't keep me in the kitchen for hours, giving me time to enjoy with my family and friends. Use them as a springboard for your own creations.

Happy cooking!

after work

Sarah's pasta with pickled anchovies

I can't take the credit for this recipe. This is my wife Sarah's quick and easy pasta to feed the kids before the babysitter arrives. My son Harry is addicted to Spanish white anchovies, which are an essential ingredient in this simple dish.

600 g tagliatelle pasta
150 g pickled white anchovies
50 g rocket
juice of 1 lemon
1 red chilli, chopped
30 ml extra virgin olive oil
salt and pepper

Bring a saucepan of salted water to the boil, add the tagliatelle and cook for about 10 minutes or until al dente. Drain.

Combine the anchovies, rocket, lemon juice, chilli and olive oil in a large bowl. Add the cooked pasta and season with salt and pepper, then gently toss together and serve.

SERVES 6

Kingfish with celeriac and chervil

My favourite type of kingfish is the Hiramasa kingfish from Spencer Gulf in South Australia. It has high levels of natural oils and fat, which keep the fish beautifully moist after it is cooked. The sharp flavour of the celeriac and subtle aniseed flavour of the chervil complete the dish. Store leftover mayonnaise dressing in an airtight container in the fridge for up to 3 days.

400 g celeriac, peeled
  and finely sliced
juice of ½ lemon
salt and pepper
½ bunch chervil, leaves picked
  and roughly chopped
extra virgin olive oil, for pan-frying
6 × 200 g kingfish fillets,
  skin removed
3 lemons, cut in half

Mayonnaise dressing
1 egg yolk
2 teaspoons white wine vinegar
1 teaspoon Dijon mustard
2 teaspoons seeded mustard
200 ml grapeseed oil
salt and pepper

Preheat the oven to 180°C.

To prepare the mayonnaise dressing, whisk together the egg yolk, white wine vinegar and mustards. Slowly drizzle in the grapeseed oil until it is absorbed, whisking constantly, then season to taste with salt and pepper. A little water can be added if you find that the consistency is too thick.

Place the celeriac in a bowl, squeeze a little lemon over the top and mix well. Season with salt and pepper, then leave to sit for 5 minutes so the celeriac can 'cook' in the lemon juice. Stir in the chopped chervil and 80 ml of the mayonnaise dressing and mix until combined.

Heat a few drops of olive oil in an ovenproof frying pan and when hot add the kingfish fillets. Cook for about 2 minutes until golden brown, then gently turn over and cook for a further 2 minutes. Transfer to the oven and cook for 3–4 minutes.

Place the celeriac salad on a plate with the kingfish fillets and serve with lemon halves.

SERVES 6

Mushroom risotto

There are two secrets to making the perfect risotto: add the stock slowly, and never stop stirring. I also add a little mascarpone at the end to give a richer flavour and a great creamy texture. Venetian cooks like to serve risotto all'onda, which literally means 'on the wave' – in other words, runny enough to flow in waves onto the plate. If you need to loosen your risotto, add half a ladle of warm stock just before you serve it. When serving, place a spoonful of risotto on the plate, then shake the plate a little to encourage it to spread towards the edges.

750 ml chicken stock
50 ml extra virgin olive oil
1 clove garlic, crushed
2 golden shallots, finely chopped
250 g risotto rice
50 ml white wine
50 g butter
50 g white oyster mushrooms,
    torn in half
50 g chestnut mushrooms,
    torn in half
50 g Swiss brown mushrooms,
    roughly sliced
50 g button mushrooms,
    roughly sliced
salt and pepper
50 g parmesan (preferably
    reggiano)
50 g mascarpone
2 teaspoons roughly chopped
    tarragon
1 tablespoon roughly chopped
    flat-leaf parsley
juice of ½ lemon

Bring the chicken stock to a simmer in a saucepan. Heat the olive oil in a heavy-based saucepan and cook the garlic and shallots for 2–3 minutes until softened. Stir in the rice until it is coated in the oil, then pour in the wine and simmer until it is completely absorbed. Add a ladle of chicken stock and stir constantly until the rice has soaked it all up. Add the remaining stock in this way, allowing the liquid to simmer but not boil.

Heat half the butter in a frying pan and sauté the mushrooms for 3–4 minutes until tender. Season with salt and pepper, then add them to the rice.

When the rice is tender and all of the stock has been absorbed, remove the saucepan from the heat. Grate the parmesan over the rice, then stir in the mascarpone, chopped herbs and remaining butter. Season with salt and pepper, give the risotto a gentle stir, then squeeze the lemon juice over the top and serve.

SERVES 6

Flathead steamed with citrus and pea shoots

All the ingredients in this nifty little dish are wrapped in a foil parcel and baked, and the resulting cooking juices become the sauce. One important tip is to make sure the parcel is tightly sealed at both ends so the fish cooks quickly and evenly. Lemon balm is a fragrant citrus-flavoured herb that works really well here – if you can't find it, use fresh mint or even basil.

240 g kipfler potatoes, peeled
butter, for greasing
4 × 175 g flathead fillets
salt and pepper
2 oranges, segmented
2 lemons, segmented
¼ bunch lemon balm, chopped
25 g pea shoots
80 g butter, extra
30 ml dry white vermouth
100 ml vegetable stock

Preheat the oven to 180°C.

Place the kipfler potatoes in a saucepan of salted water, bring to the boil and cook for 5 minutes or until tender. Drain and cut into 5 mm thick slices.

Lay out a large sheet of foil on the bench and place a piece of lightly greased baking paper on top (with the buttered side facing up). Scatter the potatoes on the paper, lay the flathead fillets on top and season with salt and pepper. Arrange the orange and lemon segments over the fillets, followed by the lemon balm and pea shoots. Finish with some knobs of butter. Bring the edges of the foil and baking paper together, then pour the vermouth and stock over the fish, fruit and vegetables. Scrunch the ends tightly to form a seal, then place on a baking tray and bake for 8 minutes. Carefully tear open the parcel and serve.

SERVES 4

Lamb rump with ratatouille and mint sauce

I grew up on a farm where we raised sheep, so I have cooked and eaten nearly every cut of lamb there is. The rump has a stronger flavour than the rack or the fillet, and a slightly chewier texture. It shines in this simplified version of a dish I serve at ARIA.

4 × 200 g lamb rump
salt and pepper
butter, for pan-frying

Mint sauce
50 g castor sugar
50 ml champagne vinegar
50 ml red wine vinegar
1 bunch mint, leaves picked,
    reserving the stalks
50 ml grapeseed oil or
    mild olive oil

Ratatouille
50 ml extra virgin olive oil
1 small red capsicum
    (pepper), diced
1 small yellow capsicum
    (pepper), diced
1 small zucchini (courgette), diced
½ small brown onion, diced
½ medium eggplant (aubergine),
    outer section only, diced
3 vine-ripened tomatoes,
    peeled and diced
salt and pepper
4 basil leaves, torn

Preheat the oven to 180°C.

To prepare the mint sauce, place the sugar and vinegars in a saucepan and boil until the sugar has dissolved. Reduce the heat to a simmer. Add the mint stalks then remove from the heat. Blanch the mint leaves in boiling water, then refresh in iced water to retain the colour. Finely chop the leaves and combine with the grapeseed oil. Just before serving, stir the mint and grapeseed oil into the vinegar mixture.

For the ratatouille, heat a little of the olive oil in a large saucepan, add the capsicum and sauté briefly, making sure it stays bright and crisp. Remove from the pan. Repeat with the zucchini, onion and eggplant, frying them separately as the cooking times for each vegetable will vary.

Combine the sautéed vegetables and chopped tomatoes in the pan and warm through for about 2 minutes. Season with salt and pepper, then add the basil just before serving.

Season the lamb rump with salt and pepper. Melt a little butter in a frying pan with an ovenproof handle, add the lamb and sear on both sides. Transfer the pan to the oven, with the lamb fat-side down, and cook for 10–15 minutes or until cooked to your liking. Remove from the oven and rest for 10 minutes.

Warm the ratatouille and spoon onto serving plates. Slice the lamb rump and place next to the ratatouille. Spoon some mint sauce over the top and serve.

SERVES 4

Lentil soup with crème fraîche

Lentils have a mild taste, which means they can carry extra flavours such as garlic, thyme, bay leaf and bacon. The crème fraîche adds a tart flavour and creamy texture at the end (use sour cream if you prefer).

25 g duck fat or
   extra virgin olive oil
2 cloves garlic, crushed
1 celery stalk, finely diced
1 brown onion, finely diced
1 carrot, finely diced
100 g speck
1 thyme sprig
1 bay leaf
250 g puy-style lentils
1.5 litres chicken stock
100 ml cream
salt and pepper
4 tablespoons crème fraîche
1 tablespoon finely chopped chives

Preheat the oven to 180°C.

Heat the duck fat or oil in an ovenproof saucepan over medium heat. Add the garlic, celery, onion and carrot and cook for 3–4 minutes until lightly coloured. Add the speck, herbs and lentils and cover with the chicken stock. Bring to the boil. Cover with a piece of greaseproof paper and a tight-fitting lid, then place the saucepan in the oven and cook for 15–20 minutes.

Remove the pan from the oven. Discard the bay leaf, thyme and speck. Mix with a hand-held blender to a smooth soup-like consistency.

Bring the soup to the boil, then stir in the cream and season to taste.

To serve, divide the soup among four bowls. Garnish with the finely chopped chives and a spoonful of crème fraîche.

SERVES 4

Veal saltimbocca

I was inspired to cook this dish at home after an episode of *The Chopping Block* where the chef of a struggling Italian restaurant had cooked the worst saltimbocca I had ever seen. The word saltimbocca means 'jump in your mouth' and I hope this version will have that effect!

800 g veal loin
salt and pepper
¼ bunch sage, leaves picked
12 slices provolone cheese
12 slices prosciutto
extra virgin olive oil,
    for pan-frying
50 g butter
1 lemon, cut into quarters
rocket, to serve

Preheat the oven to 120°C.

Trim any fat or sinew from the outside of the veal loin, then cut the loin into six pieces and place on a chopping board. Beat the veal with a meat mallet until each piece is approximately 5 mm thick. Season the veal and place the sage leaves on top. Sandwich each piece of veal between two slices of provolone cheese, then wrap in prosciutto.

Heat a little oil in a large non-stick frying pan. Working in batches, add the wrapped veal to the pan and cook over high heat for 1–2 minutes or until the prosciutto is crispy, then turn over and cook the other side. Add the butter to the pan and cook for a further 1 minute, then squeeze some lemon juice over the veal. Keep warm in the oven while you cook the rest.

To serve, arrange some rocket on warmed plates. Place the veal alongside the rocket and spoon a little of the butter from the pan over the top. Serve immediately.

SERVES 6

Orecchiette with cauliflower, mint, peas and breadcrumbs

Orecchiette are pasta discs made in the shape of little ears. They work really well with chunky vegetable and meat-based sauces. When I make this recipe at home, I cut the cauliflower to a similar size to the orecchiette so the two ingredients come together as one in this rustic pasta dish. Japanese panko breadcrumbs are great for when you don't have time to make your own from day-old bread – they're available from most supermarkets.

100 ml extra virgin olive oil
50 g Japanese panko breadcrumbs
400 g orecchiette pasta
150 g peas
½ cauliflower, cut into
    small florets
salt and pepper
2 cloves garlic, thinly sliced
75 g butter
60 g pecorino, shaved
¼ bunch mint, cut into
    thin strips

Heat 70 ml olive oil in a saucepan and lightly brown the breadcrumbs. Remove and drain on kitchen paper.

Bring a saucepan of salted water to the boil, add the orecchiette and cook for about 12 minutes or until al dente. Blanch the peas in boiling water for 30 seconds.

Meanwhile, heat the remaining olive oil in a large frying pan, add the cauliflower florets and season with salt and pepper. Cook for 6–7 minutes or until golden brown. Add the sliced garlic, then stir in the blanched peas and cook for a further minute.

Drain the pasta, reserving a couple of spoonfuls of the cooking liquid, then add the pasta to the frying pan with the cauliflower and peas. Add the butter and half the cheese and toss through until melted. Season with salt and pepper. Add a little of the reserved cooking liquid if you think the pasta looks a bit dry. Stir in the breadcrumbs and mint, then serve with the remaining cheese.

SERVES 6

Snapper with cauliflower and broccolini

This is a quick and easy dish that I cook at home to make sure the kids eat their fair share of vegetables. If you like, serve it on a dollop of creamy puréed potatoes or celeriac.

120 g cauliflower
100 g broccolini
20 ml extra virgin olive oil, plus
    extra for drizzling
4 × 160 g snapper fillets
60 g butter, diced
100 g chanterelle mushrooms
2 golden shallots, finely chopped
1 tablespoon chopped chives
20 g toasted pine nuts
1 lemon, cut into wedges

Preheat the oven to 180°C.

Remove the florets from the broccolini and cauliflower and blanch in salted boiling water. Refresh in iced water, then drain.

Heat the oil in an ovenproof frying pan. Add the snapper fillets, skin-side down, and cook for 2–3 minutes until golden. Place in the oven for 4 minutes, then remove and allow to rest.

Wipe the frying pan clean. Melt the butter in the clean pan, then sauté the mushrooms, shallots, cauliflower and broccolini for 2–3 minutes until golden and cooked through. Stir in the chives and pine nuts.

To serve, spoon a pile of vegetables onto each plate then place a snapper fillet alongside. Drizzle with a little olive oil and serve with lemon wedges.

SERVES 4

Parmesan-crumbed veal cutlet

This is a weeknight regular at my house – it's easy to make and a real crowd pleaser. I usually have a loaf of sourdough bread hanging around that I make into breadcrumbs, but you can also use Japanese panko breadcrumbs, which are available at most supermarkets. Serve with a rocket salad and Mashed potato (see page 158).

6 veal cutlets
3 egg yolks
200 ml milk
100 g fresh or Japanese panko
   breadcrumbs
50 g parmesan (preferably
   reggiano), grated
100 g plain flour, for dusting
salt and pepper
100 ml extra virgin olive oil
20 g butter
handful flat-leaf parsley,
   leaves picked
2 lemons, cut into wedges

Preheat the oven to 120°C.

Place the veal cutlets between two pieces of plastic film and pat them out with a meat mallet to a thickness of 1–1.5 cm.

Whisk the egg yolks and milk together until combined. In a separate bowl, mix the breadcrumbs and parmesan together.

Lightly dust the veal cutlets with flour. Dip them into the egg and milk mixture, then coat with the breadcrumbs and parmesan. Season with salt and pepper.

Heat the olive oil in a large frying pan, add the cutlets in batches and cook for 2–3 minutes. Turn the cutlets over, add the butter and cook for a further 2–3 minutes until golden. Remove and drain on kitchen paper. Keep warm in the oven while you cook the rest, then serve with parsley and lemon wedges.

SERVES 6

Roast sweet potato and tzatziki

I make this side dish a lot at home and usually serve it with Barbecue chicken with chermoula rub (see page 101). Sweet potatoes naturally have a high sugar content, making them susceptible to burning. To prevent this, turn them over a few times while they are roasting.

1 kg sweet potatoes
4 cloves garlic, crushed
  in their skins
80 ml extra virgin olive oil
1 thyme sprig
1 rosemary sprig
salt and pepper

Tzatziki
200 g Greek yoghurt
1 clove garlic, chopped
¼ bunch coriander, chopped
salt and pepper
1 long cucumber

Preheat the oven to 200°C. Peel the sweet potatoes and cut into 1 cm thick rounds. Place in a roasting tin with the garlic, olive oil, thyme, rosemary and seasoning and bake for about 30 minutes until tender (the bottoms should be golden brown), turning them every so often.

To make the tzatziki, pour the yoghurt into a bowl and add the garlic, coriander and seasoning. Grate the cucumber into the yoghurt and mix well.

To serve, arrange the sweet potato slices on a plate and spoon the tzatziki over the top.

SERVES 6

Tempura garfish with peas and zucchini

This simple dish features the contrasting textures of crisp battered fish and glazed peas and zucchini. If you can't find garfish fillets, use another small white-fleshed fish such as sand whiting or flathead. A bowl of lemon wedges is all you need as an accompaniment.

3 tablespoons extra virgin olive oil
15 g butter
½ leek, well-washed, cut into
    quarters and chopped
1 clove garlic, chopped
30 ml chicken or vegetable stock
30 ml white wine
2 medium kipfler potatoes,
    cut into 1 cm dice
100 g peas
1 zucchini (courgette), sliced
vegetable oil, for deep-frying
12 medium garfish fillets

Tempura batter
100 g plain flour
50 g cornflour
25 g baking powder
250 ml iced water
1 teaspoon salt

To prepare the tempura batter, place all the ingredients in a bowl and whisk to a thin batter consistency.

Heat the olive oil and butter in a frying pan over medium heat, add the leek and garlic and sauté for 4–6 minutes or until the leek is translucent. Pour in the stock and white wine and simmer for 3–4 minutes until most of the liquid has evaporated and the mixture is quite dry. Add the potato and cook for 3–4 minutes, then stir in the peas and zucchini and cook for a further 2–3 minutes until the vegetables are tender.

Half-fill a deep-fryer or heavy-based frying pan with vegetable oil and heat to 170°C (a cube of bread dropped in the oil should brown in 20 seconds).

Coat each fish fillet in the batter. Working in batches, carefully lower the fillets into the hot oil and cook for 2–3 minutes until golden brown. Remove and drain on kitchen paper.

To serve, place the sautéed vegetables in a bowl and arrange the tempura garfish fillets on top.

SERVES 4

Roast fennel with borlotti beans

This is one of my favourite sides to serve in winter – it's one of those dishes that tastes even better the next day, once all the flavours have settled and combined. It works particularly well with roast chicken or whole roast fish such as snapper.

100 g butter
1 carrot, peeled and chopped
1 brown onion, chopped
1 head garlic, cut in half
300 g fresh borlotti beans
1 litre vegetable stock
50 ml extra virgin olive oil,
    plus extra to serve
2 tomatoes, peeled,
    seeded and diced
80 g green olives, pitted
    and torn
salt and pepper
2 tablespoons roughly
    chopped flat-leaf parsley

Roast fennel
20 ml extra virgin olive oil
4 fennel bulbs, trimmed
    and cut in half
salt and pepper
2 litres vegetable stock
    or water

Preheat the oven to 150°C.

Melt the butter in a large saucepan and sauté the carrot, onion and garlic. Add the borlotti beans and pour in enough vegetable stock to cover. Bring to the boil, then transfer to an ovenproof dish and braise in the oven for about 1 hour or until tender. Remove from the oven and allow to cool in the liquid. Leave the oven on for the fennel.

Heat the olive oil in a frying pan, add the tomatoes and olives and season with salt and pepper. Stir in the borlotti bean mixture and cook for 3–4 minutes, then stir in the parsley.

To prepare the roast fennel, heat the olive oil in a deep roasting tin over medium heat. When hot, add the fennel halves, cut-side down, and cook for about 3–4 minutes until they begin to brown. Season with salt and pepper, then cover with the stock or water and cook in the oven for about 20 minutes until tender.

Place the fennel in the centre of each serving plate and surround with the borlotti beans, tomatoes and olives. Drizzle a little olive oil over the top and serve.

SERVES 4

Peter Bracher's eggplant meatballs

This recipe is from my brother-in-law Peter, who is a very keen and capable cook. The key ingredient here is the eggplant purée, which keeps the meatballs perfectly soft and moist. You can also use the mixture to make traditional meatballs, served with homemade tomato sauce and spaghetti.

1.5 kg eggplants (aubergines)
500 g minced lean lamb
3 eggs, lightly beaten
salt and pepper
plain flour, for dusting
extra virgin olive oil,
   for pan-frying
juice of 1 lemon
Gremolata, to serve
   (see page 70)

Preheat the barbecue to its hottest setting or place a chargrill pan over high heat. Grill the whole eggplants for about 15 minutes until blackened, turning as required. Remove from the heat and allow to cool slightly, then peel the skin away from the flesh. Place the eggplant flesh in a sieve to drain as much liquid as possible, then finely dice and place in a large bowl.

Add the minced lamb and beaten egg to the eggplant and season with salt and pepper. Mix together with your hands, then form into walnut-sized balls. Slightly flatten the balls with your hands, then dust lightly with flour.

Heat some olive oil in a frying pan over high heat, then carefully add some of the meatballs, taking care not to overcrowd the pan. Fry the meatballs for 7–8 minutes until golden brown, turning occasionally. Remove and drain on kitchen paper. Repeat the process until all the meatballs are cooked.

Squeeze a little lemon juice over the eggplant meatballs and serve with some gremolata.

SERVES 8

Blue-eye trevalla hot pot

This dish is a favourite of mine from the days when my business partner Peter Sullivan and I owned our first restaurant, the Paddington Inn Bistro. When I cook it at home, I serve it with rice or couscous, and perhaps some braised chickpeas, diced tomatoes with mint and a bowl of plain yoghurt on the side.

20 ml extra virgin olive oil

6 × 200 g blue-eye trevalla fillets

½ bunch flat-leaf parsley, leaves picked and chopped

½ bunch coriander, chopped

2 cloves garlic, very finely chopped

250 g mango chutney (preferably Sharwood's)

1 small chilli, finely chopped

1 teaspoon chopped ginger

2 teaspoons cumin seeds, roasted and ground into a powder

2 teaspoons coriander seeds, roasted and ground into a powder

500 ml chicken stock

75 g roasted pine nuts

pinch saffron threads

salt and pepper

1 lemon

Heat the olive oil in a large frying pan over high heat. When hot, add the fish fillets, skin-side down, and cook for 3–4 minutes until golden brown.

Place the remaining ingredients (except the lemon) in a large saucepan, mix well and bring to the boil. Add the fish fillets to the pan, skin-side up, then cover and cook for a further 5 minutes.

Place the fillets in the middle of serving plates and spoon the sauce over the top. Squeeze a little lemon juice over the top and serve with rice or couscous.

SERVES 6

Steamed mussels

Steamed mussels would have to be the simplest one-pot dish around. These days, you can buy farmed black mussels that have already been debearded to make cooking them even easier. My tip is not to throw out any mussels that have not opened. Despite what many people think, unopened mussels are not off; they just need a little extra cooking time. When all of the mussels are ready, place the saucepan in the middle of the table with some bowls, crusty bread and a bowl of homemade mayonnaise.

1 small leek, well-washed
   and chopped
1 small brown onion, chopped
1 long red chilli, chopped
¼ bunch flat-leaf parsley,
   leaves picked and chopped
2 cloves garlic, crushed
3 kg mussels, scrubbed
   and debearded
100 ml extra virgin olive oil
300 ml white wine
2 bay leaves

Combine the leek, onion, chilli, parsley and garlic in a bowl. Add the mussels and toss through.

Heat the olive oil in a large heavy-based saucepan. When the oil begins to smoke, add the mussels and leek mixture, wine and bay leaves. Cover and steam for 2–3 minutes until all the mussels are open. Transfer to a large bowl or serve straight from the pan.

SERVES 6

Marinated sardines

Sardines are a really underrated fish, possibly because there is such a large range of inferior tinned sardines available that people don't realise how good the fresh version can be. This recipe doesn't really cook them in the traditional sense, but the lemon juice pickles the sardines so they are ready to eat. Serve with chargrilled sourdough bread on the side.

12 sardine fillets
juice of 1 lemon
1 teaspoon sea salt
1 small red chilli, finely chopped
1 clove garlic, sliced
¼ bunch coriander, leaves picked
salt and pepper
60 ml extra virgin olive oil
rocket, to serve
1 lemon, cut into 6 wedges

Marinate the sardines in the lemon juice and sea salt for 15 minutes. Add the chilli, garlic and coriander and season to taste. Cover with the extra virgin olive oil, then serve on a bed of rocket with lemon wedges.

SERVES 6

at the weekend

Red onion and gruyère focaccia

I must admit I don't make bread at home very often, but when I do I keep coming back to this recipe. While the preparation time is fairly short, the starter needs at least 12 hours to develop and the dough needs about 90 minutes to prove. You can use the proving time to organise the other elements of the meal.

1 red onion, sliced
70 g gruyère, grated
3 thyme sprigs, leaves picked
generous pinch sea salt
30 ml extra virgin olive oil

Starter
150 ml water
2.5 g dried yeast
125 g bakers' flour

Dough
200 ml water
12.5 g dried yeast
275 g bakers' flour
pinch salt
20 ml extra virgin olive oil

To prepare the starter, pour the water into a bowl and sprinkle the yeast into it. Stir to dissolve, then leave for 5 minutes until it starts to foam. Add the flour and mix together to form a batter. Cover with a tea towel and leave to ferment for 12–36 hours.

To make the dough, pour half the water into a bowl and sprinkle the yeast into it. Stir to dissolve, then leave for 5 minutes. Mix together the flour and salt in a large bowl, make a well and pour in the yeasted water, olive oil and starter. Mix the flour and liquids together and stir in the remaining water to form a sticky dough (add a little extra water if necessary). Turn out onto a floured work surface and knead the dough for about 10 minutes until smooth.

Place the dough in an oiled bowl and cover with a tea towel. Leave in a warm place for about 1½ hours or until the dough has doubled in size. Knock it back and knead for another 5 minutes, then leave to rest for a further 10 minutes.

Roll out the dough on a lightly floured surface to form a circle about 24 cm in diameter. Place the dough on an oiled baking tray and cover with a tea towel. Leave the dough to prove for about 20 minutes or until it has doubled in size.

Preheat the oven to 200°C.

Gently press your fingertips into the dough, making dimples about 1 cm deep. Scatter the onion and gruyère on top, then sprinkle with thyme and salt. Drizzle with the olive oil.

Bake for about 30 minutes until the focaccia has risen and the topping is crisp. Cool slightly on a wire rack, then cut into wedges and serve warm.

SERVES 6

Seafood linguine

Most of the work in this dish is in the preparation of the seafood. After that, it is simply cooked and added to al dente pasta. Feel free to add whatever seafood looks fresh on the day, such as vongole or Moreton Bay bugs.

12 raw king prawns
500 g linguine
1 kg mussels, scrubbed
   and debearded
50 ml white wine
40 ml extra virgin olive oil
2 red chillies, finely chopped
4 cloves garlic, finely chopped
300 g squid, cleaned and
   cut into 1 cm strips
¼ bunch flat-leaf parsley,
   leaves picked and
   finely chopped
10 g butter
juice of 1 lemon

Peel the prawns and remove the heads and tails. Run a sharp knife along the spine of each prawn, making a small incision to remove the vein. Cut the prawns in half lengthways and set aside.

Bring a saucepan of salted water to the boil, add the linguine and cook for 8–10 minutes until al dente.

Rinse the mussels and place in a large saucepan with the white wine. Cover with a lid and cook over high heat for 3–4 minutes or until the mussels have opened. Reserve the wine and remove the meat from the shells.

Heat 20 ml of the olive oil in a large frying pan and gently sauté the chilli and garlic for 2 minutes or until translucent. In a separate frying pan, heat the remaining olive oil, add the squid and prawns and sauté for 2 minutes. Add the mussels and chopped parsley and cook for 1 minute to warm through. Stir in the reserved wine to deglaze the pan and cook for a further minute.

Strain the linguine and add to the frying pan with the chilli and garlic oil. Add the butter and toss through until the pasta is evenly coated. Divide the linguine among six bowls and place the squid, prawns and mussels on top. Squeeze over the lemon juice and serve.

SERVES 6

Baby capsicums stuffed with ratatouille

Most good fruit and vegetable stores sell these shiny little red and yellow capsicums. If you can't find them, use regular capsicums and cut them in half. As the capsicums roast away in the oven their natural sweet flavour takes over, making them the perfect vegetable to fill with ratatouille. This dish can be served with pesto and salad leaves as a starter, or with a roasted rack of lamb for main course.

12 baby capsicums (peppers)
20 ml extra virgin olive oil
salt and pepper
200 g sea salt
150 ml vegetable oil
1 red capsicum (pepper),
    seeded and diced
1 yellow capsicum (pepper),
    seeded and diced
1 zucchini (courgette), finely diced
1 eggplant (aubergine), finely diced
3 vine-ripened tomatoes, peeled,
    seeded and finely diced

Preheat the oven to 175°C.

Cut the baby capsicums in half lengthways and scoop out the core to form the casing for the ratatouille. Toss the capsicums in a little olive oil and season with salt and pepper.

Spread the sea salt on a baking tray and place the capsicums on top, cut-side up, in a single layer. Bake for 5–10 minutes until they have softened a little but are not cooked through.

Heat the vegetable oil in a frying pan and sauté the diced capsicum, zucchini and eggplant for 2 minutes. Allow to cool, then mix the vegetables with the diced tomato and season with salt and pepper. Fill each baby capsicum with the ratatouille and serve.

SERVES 6

Salt-crusted chicken

This recipe is a different take on traditional roast chicken. Here, the chicken is encased in a salt pastry and roasted in the oven. The flavours of the herbs and salt permeate the chicken to give it a unique, tangy flavour.

2 tablespoons coriander seeds
¼ bunch rosemary, leaves picked
and finely chopped
¼ bunch thyme, leaves picked
and finely chopped
¼ bunch sage, leaves picked
and finely chopped
2 bay leaves
1.5 kg sea salt
grated zest of 2 lemons
200 ml water
1 × 1.6 kg chicken

Preheat the oven to 200°C.

Crush the coriander seeds using a mortar and pestle. Place the crushed seeds, herbs, salt, lemon zest and water in a food processor and mix until all ingredients are combined.

Spread the salt mixture over the whole chicken to form a 5 mm layer over the outside.

Place in a roasting tin and roast for 1–1¼ hours or until the chicken is cooked through. Check by inserting a skewer into the leg – it should be warm to touch when removed. Serve with roast potatoes and steamed vegetables or a crisp green salad.

SERVES 4

Gnocchi with roast pumpkin, sage and pecorino

I love this combination of nutty fried gnocchi, caramelised pumpkin and the herbal flavour of fried sage. I like to use pecorino cheese to finish this dish but if you only have parmesan in the fridge, that will work just as well.

½ butternut pumpkin,
    peeled, seeded and
    cut into 1 cm dice
iced water, for refreshing
30 ml vegetable oil
salt and pepper
30 g butter, diced
½ bunch sage, leaves picked
30 g pecorino, grated

Gnocchi
rock salt, for baking
1.5 kg pontiac potatoes
150 g plain flour
2 egg yolks
salt
extra virgin olive oil,
    for tossing

Preheat the oven to 180°C.

To prepare the gnocchi, spread a layer of rock salt on a baking tray and place the potatoes on top. Bake for about 40 minutes until the potatoes are tender. Scrape out the soft flesh, mash it, then pass through a sieve. Add the flour, egg yolks and a good pinch of salt and work into a dough on the benchtop. Roll the dough into a sausage shape (approximately 2 cm in diameter) and cut into 2 cm pieces.

Bring a large saucepan of salted water to the boil, add the gnocchi and cook until they rise to the surface (this will only take a minute or so). Remove the gnocchi with a slotted spoon and refresh in iced water. Drain, then toss with a little olive oil.

Blanch the pumpkin in a saucepan of salted, boiling water for about 5 minutes. Remove and refresh in iced water, then drain.

Heat the vegetable oil in a frying pan, add the pumpkin and season with salt and pepper. Cook over medium heat for about 3 minutes until the pumpkin is caramelised, then remove. Add the gnocchi to the same pan and caramelise until golden. Season to taste. Stir in the diced butter until it starts to turn a nutty brown colour, then add the sage and remove from the heat.

To serve, arrange the gnocchi and pumpkin on plates. Drizzle the butter over the top and garnish with the sage leaves and freshly grated pecorino.

SERVES 6

Caramelised onion, radicchio and gorgonzola
pizza
When I make pizzas at home, I like to get the kids involved. They help me knead the dough (although some of it seems to become edible playdough!) and place the ingredients on top. This pizza makes use of radicchio, a favourite lettuce of many Italians.

20 g dried yeast
200 ml warm water
40 ml white wine
50 ml olive oil
445 g bakers' flour
1 tablespoon salt
200 g butter
2 brown onions, sliced
70 g gorgonzola, crumbled
½ radicchio lettuce, shredded

Dissolve the yeast in the warm water, then mix with the wine, olive oil, flour and salt to form a dough. Knead for about 5 minutes or until the dough is smooth. Place the dough in a large oiled bowl, cover with a tea towel and leave in a warm place for about 1½ hours until it doubles in size. Knock it back, knead again briefly, then cut the dough in half and roll out on a lightly floured surface to form two 30 cm circles.

Preheat the oven to 250°C.

Melt the butter in a frying pan over low heat and cook the onion slowly until it turns golden brown. Scatter the cooked onion over the pizza bases and top with the crumbled gorgonzola. Bake for 10 minutes.

Top with the shredded radicchio and serve immediately.

SERVES 2

Fried school prawns with aïoli

In my opinion, there is nothing better to eat on a hot summer's afternoon than fresh school prawns. Two bits of advice: cook the prawns in small batches so the temperature of the oil doesn't drop, and make sure you use an oil with a neutral flavour, such as cottonseed or grapeseed oil.

vegetable oil, for deep-frying
100 g plain flour
salt and pepper
600 g raw school prawns
3 bunches flat-leaf parsley
2 lemons, cut into wedges

Quick aïoli
100 g mayonnaise
½ clove garlic, crushed
juice of ½ lemon
salt and pepper

To prepare the aïoli, mix together the mayonnaise, garlic and lemon juice then season with salt and pepper. Cover and leave to infuse in the refrigerator for at least an hour, then remove from the fridge and pass through a fine sieve.

Half-fill a deep-fryer or heavy-based frying pan with oil and heat to 180°C (a cube of bread dropped in the oil should brown in 15 seconds).

Season the flour with salt and pepper. Toss the prawns through the flour, then carefully lower them into the hot oil. Cook for about 1 minute, then remove and drain on kitchen paper. Season to taste with salt.

Place small bunches of parsley in the hot oil and cook for 10 seconds until golden brown and crunchy. Remove and drain on kitchen paper.

To serve, place the prawns and deep-fried parsley in a large bowl. Serve with the aïoli and lemon wedges.

SERVES 6

Poached chicken in master stock

This is a dish I cook at home more than any other – the chicken cooks slowly by steeping in the master stock, giving it a wonderfully moist texture. I have had my own master stock in the freezer for nearly nine years and it develops more and more flavour every time it is used. After you use it to cook your chicken, bring it to the boil, skim any froth off the top, then let it cool to room temperature and freeze it for next time.

1 × 1.8 kg chicken
2 bunches baby bok choy

Master stock
1.6 litres chicken stock
330 ml light soy sauce
200 ml rice wine vinegar
200 g castor sugar
5 cm knob ginger,
  roughly chopped
2 star anise
3 cinnamon quills
60 ml sherry vinegar
2 small chillies, cut in half
1 orange, peel only
1 bunch coriander, roots only

Spring onion and ginger mix
4 spring onions, finely chopped
1 tablespoon finely chopped ginger
½ clove garlic, finely chopped
20 ml peanut oil
2 teaspoons sea salt
20 ml rice wine vinegar
freshly ground black pepper

Combine all the ingredients for the spring onion and ginger mix in a bowl.

To prepare the master stock, place all the ingredients in a stockpot and simmer for 20 minutes. Bring to the boil and add the whole chicken, then reduce the heat and simmer for a further 5 minutes. Turn off the heat, cover with the lid and leave for 1½ hours.

When ready to serve, blanch the bok choy in salted, boiling water for 30 seconds, then refresh in iced water.

Cut the chicken into pieces and serve with the bok choy, the spring onion and ginger mix, and some steamed rice.

SERVES 4

Asian greens with tsuyu sauce

This side dish was inspired by countless late-night visits to my favourite Japanese teppanyaki restaurant after service. We'd feast on platters of tiny pieces of grilled beef, fish and chicken, steamed rice and, of course, Asian green vegetables. I like to use at least three different vegetables to provide a contrast in flavour and texture – although make sure the leafy vegetables such as bok choy are cleaned under plenty of running water to remove hidden dirt and grit. The recipe for the dressing was given to me by one of our sous chefs, Kazu, who is originally from Japan. Tsuyu sauce is traditionally a noodle dipping sauce but is great served with Asian vegetables. This recipe makes a delicious accompaniment for Poached chicken in master stock (see previous page).

6 bunches bok choy
1 bunch choy sum
2 bunches garlic chives
2 bunches gai larn
   (Chinese broccoli)
1 teaspoon sesame seeds

Tsuyu sauce
150 ml chicken stock
1 teaspoon bonito flakes
40 ml soy sauce
40 ml mirin
¾ teaspoon castor sugar
½ teaspoon wasabi powder
½ teaspoon sesame oil

To prepare the tsuyu sauce, place the chicken stock and bonito in a saucepan and bring to the boil. Simmer for 20 minutes. Add the soy sauce, mirin, castor sugar, wasabi powder and sesame oil and bring back to the boil. Remove from the heat and strain through a fine sieve.

Blanch the bok choy, choy sum, garlic chives and gai larn by placing them in a large saucepan of boiling salted water and simmering for 1 minute.

Drain the vegetables and arrange on a serving plate. Stir the tsuyu sauce well and pour over the vegetables. Garnish with the sesame seeds and serve.

SERVES 6

Lamb broth with pearl barley and fennel

Pearl barley is well suited to this old-fashioned style of broth. It is paired with braised lamb neck which gives the soup that distinctive sweet lamb flavour. I like to soak the pearl barley in cold water overnight, to give a fluffier texture and reduce the cooking time.

2 lamb necks, boned
salt and pepper
50 ml vegetable oil
1 brown onion, thinly sliced
1 large fennel bulb, trimmed
   and thinly sliced
1 tablespoon fennel seeds
2 cloves garlic, peeled and
   cut in half
50 ml white wine
3 litres chicken stock
100 g pearl barley, soaked
   overnight
1 head curly kale

Preheat the oven to 140°C.

Cut the lamb into 2 cm slices and season with salt and pepper. Heat half the oil in a frying pan and cook the lamb for 2–3 minutes, turning occasionally until golden brown.

In a separate ovenproof saucepan, heat the remaining oil and cook the onion, fennel, fennel seeds and garlic until lightly coloured. Add the white wine and cook for a further 1–2 minutes. Stir in the lamb, then pour in the chicken stock to cover and bring to the boil. Skim off any fat and place the lid on the saucepan.

Cook in the oven for 1 hour, then remove from the oven and add the drained pearl barley. Stir gently and return to the oven for another 30 minutes. Add the curly kale, allow it to wilt, then serve immediately.

SERVES 6

Roast baby chickens with gnocchi, treviso and mushrooms

When I cook baby chickens, I always remove the backbone and flatten them out so the marinade can completely flavour the bird. The other advantage is that they will cook much faster this way.

6 baby chickens
2 cloves garlic, chopped
¼ bunch thyme, leaves picked
grated zest and juice of 1 lemon
100 ml olive oil
salt and pepper
30 g butter
80 g oyster mushrooms,
    trimmed and cut in half
80 g chestnut mushrooms,
    trimmed and cut in half
80 g king brown mushrooms,
    trimmed and cut in half
1 treviso lettuce or radicchio,
    leaves washed and torn
    into pieces

Gnocchi with marjoram
1 kg pontiac potatoes
¼ bunch marjoram, leaves
    picked and chopped
250 g plain flour
2 egg yolks
salt and pepper
olive oil

To prepare the chickens, remove the backbone by cutting along the back with a knife. Spread the body cavity on a flat surface and press firmly to flatten. Combine the garlic, thyme, lemon zest, half the lemon juice and half the olive oil. Season with salt and pepper, then pour over the birds and leave to marinate for at least an hour.

Preheat the oven to 180°C.

To prepare the gnocchi, bake the potatoes in their skins for about 1 hour or until soft. Remove the potatoes but leave the oven on for the chicken. Scrape the potato flesh from its skin, mash, then pass through a sieve. Combine the marjoram, flour, egg yolks, salt and pepper with the potato and work into a dough. Roll the dough into a sausage shape (about 2 cm in diameter), then cut the dough into 2 cm wide discs.

Cook the gnocchi in salted boiling water for 1–2 minutes or until they rise to the surface. Scoop out and refresh in iced water, then drain. Toss with a little olive oil and refrigerate until required.

Heat a little olive oil in a frying pan. Add the chickens, skin-side down, and cook for 2–3 minutes until golden brown, then turn over and repeat. You will need to do this in batches. Remove the chickens from the pan and place in a roasting tin. Place the tin in the oven and cook the birds for a further 10 minutes. To check if they are cooked, pierce the thigh with the tip of a sharp knife – the juices should run clear.

While the birds are cooking, heat the remaining olive oil in a large non-stick frying pan. Add the gnocchi and cook for about 2 minutes until golden brown. Add the butter and mushrooms, season with salt and pepper and cook for a further 2 minutes. Add the treviso leaves and cook for 1 minute until the leaves begin to wilt, then add a few drops of lemon juice to taste.

Remove the baby chickens from the oven, cut them in half and serve on top of the gnocchi, mushrooms and treviso leaves.

SERVES 6

Fig and jamón bruschetta

Give me figs, jamón (Spanish ham) and good-quality balsamic vinegar and I am a happy man! This bruschetta is all about simply letting great ingredients speak for themselves.

6 black figs, cut into quarters

60 g jamón, sliced and
    torn into pieces

20 g rocket

salt and pepper

6 slices sourdough bread

60 ml extra virgin olive oil

1 clove garlic, peeled and
    cut in half

Balsamic dressing

60 ml extra virgin olive oil

30 ml balsamic vinegar

To prepare the dressing, whisk together the extra virgin olive oil and balsamic vinegar.

Mix together the figs, jamón and rocket. Season with salt and pepper.

Drizzle each side of the bread slices with a little olive oil, then chargrill or cook under a hot grill until golden brown. While the bread is still warm, rub the garlic over each side of the bread.

To serve, dress the fig mixture with the balsamic dressing and place on the grilled sourdough.

SERVES 6

Orange and fennel bruschetta

The aniseed flavour of fennel blends well with citrus, especially orange, and makes an appealing vegetarian snack.

6 slices sourdough bread

60 ml extra virgin olive oil

1 clove garlic, peeled and
    cut in half

3 oranges, segmented

2 fennel bulbs, trimmed and
    thinly sliced

fennel fronds, chopped

Lemon and orange dressing

60 ml extra virgin olive oil

1 teaspoon sugar

salt and pepper

3 teaspoons lemon juice

3 teaspoons orange juice

To prepare the dressing, whisk together all the ingredients until combined.

Drizzle each side of the bread slices with a little olive oil, then chargrill or cook under a hot grill or until golden brown. While the bread is still warm, rub the garlic over each side of the bread.

Mix together the orange segments, sliced fennel and fennel fronds, and dress with the lemon and orange dressing. Place the salad on the grilled sourdough and serve.

SERVES 6

Clockwise from top left: Fig and jamón bruschetta, Orange and fennel bruschetta, Tomato and basil bruschetta (recipe on next page) and Cannellini and broad bean bruschetta (recipe on next page)

Tomato and basil bruschetta
For this (pictured on previous page), use the plumpest, reddest tomatoes, really fresh basil and mild, sweet-tasting red onion.

6 slices sourdough bread
100 ml extra virgin olive oil
1 clove garlic, peeled and
    cut in half
6 small vine-ripened tomatoes,
    cut into 5 mm thick slices
¼ red onion, very thinly sliced
¼ bunch basil, leaves picked and
    finely shredded
salt and pepper
2 teaspoons balsamic vinegar

Drizzle each side of the bread slices with a little olive oil, then chargrill or cook under a hot grill until golden brown. While the bread is still warm, rub the garlic over each side of the bread.

Arrange the tomato slices on the grilled sourdough. Top with the red onion and the shredded basil. Season with salt and pepper. Drizzle the remaining olive oil and a few drops of balsamic vinegar over the top and serve.

SERVES 6

Cannellini and broad bean bruschetta
In winter I look for any excuse to use fresh broad beans. In this recipe (pictured on previous page) I have combined them with cannellini beans, cherry tomatoes and anchovies.

150 g dried cannellini beans
100 g broad beans
6 cherry tomatoes, cut into
    quarters
40 ml extra virgin olive oil,
    plus extra for drizzling
20 ml red wine vinegar
salt and pepper
6 slices sourdough bread
1 clove garlic, peeled and
    cut in half
6 anchovy fillets, cut into strips

Place the cannellini beans in a saucepan, cover with water and bring to the boil. Reduce the heat and simmer for about 20 minutes or until tender. Drain.

Remove the broad beans from their pods. Bring a saucepan of salted water to the boil, add the broad beans and blanch for 1 minute. Drain and refresh in iced water, then drain again and slip off the outer shells.

In a large bowl, mix together the cannellini beans, broad beans, cherry tomatoes, olive oil and red wine vinegar, then season with salt and pepper.

Drizzle each side of the bread slices with a little olive oil, then chargrill or cook under a hot grill until golden brown. While the bread is still warm, rub the garlic over each side of the bread.

To serve, spoon the bean and tomato mixture onto the grilled sourdough and arrange anchovy strips on top.

SERVES 6

Vegetable stock
The weekend is a great time to cook up a batch of stock to keep in the freezer, ready for the next time you want to make soup or risotto.

100 g butter
3 carrots, finely chopped
2 brown onions, finely chopped
1 leek, finely chopped
1 small fennel bulb, finely chopped
1 head celery, finely chopped
1 tarragon sprig
3 cloves garlic, chopped
1 thyme sprig
1 bay leaf
1 tablespoon coriander
    seeds, crushed
300 ml white wine
salt and pepper
½ bunch basil
½ bunch flat-leaf parsley
½ bunch chervil

Place the butter in a large saucepan or stockpot with all of the vegetables and cook for 3–4 minutes until the onions are translucent. Add the garlic, thyme, bay leaves, crushed coriander seeds and white wine and cook for 2 minutes.

Pour in about 4 litres of water and bring to the boil. Cook for a further 10 minutes then season to taste with salt and pepper.

Remove from the heat and add the basil, parsley and chervil. Leave the stock to sit for 15 minutes then pass through a fine sieve. Allow to cool and use as required.

MAKES ABOUT 3 LITRES

Chicken stock
This simple stock can be stored in the refrigerator for up to 4 days or frozen for several months.

2.5 kg chicken bones or wings
1 onion, roughly chopped
3 celery stalks, roughly chopped
2 leeks, roughly chopped
1 head garlic, cut in half crossways
1 bunch thyme
2 bay leaves
10 white peppercorns

Place the chicken bones or wings in a large saucepan or stockpot and cover with water. Bring to the boil and skim off any impurities. Reduce the heat to low and add the chopped vegetables, garlic, thyme, bay leaves and peppercorns. Simmer for 4 hours, skimming occasionally, then strain through a fine sieve and allow to cool.

For a stronger stock, this light stock can be simmered until reduced by half.

MAKES ABOUT 2 LITRES

Chicken and vegetable soup

This is a hearty rustic broth that I cook a few times every winter when someone in my family has succumbed to the dreaded flu. Using a whole chicken adds an intense chicken flavour. Of course, you don't have to be unwell to enjoy this soup – it is the perfect evening meal.

70 g butter
30 ml extra virgin olive oil
2 carrots, diced
1 medium white onion, diced
1 leek, white part only,
   well-washed and diced
1 celery stalk, trimmed and diced
1 clove garlic, chopped
1 teaspoon chopped thyme
1 teaspoon chopped rosemary
50 ml wine
1 × 1.6 kg chicken, washed
   and jointed
1.5 litres chicken stock
salt and pepper
½ punnet baby beans, sliced
1 bunch asparagus, sliced
¼ bunch chervil, chopped
½ bunch flat-leaf parsley,
   leaves picked and chopped
2 tarragon sprigs, leaves only

Pistou
½ bunch basil, leaves picked
30 g grated parmesan
   (preferably reggiano)
30 g pine nuts, toasted
1 small clove garlic, peeled
40 ml olive oil

Heat the butter and oil in a large saucepan, add the carrot, onion, leek, celery, garlic, thyme and rosemary and cook for 3–4 minutes until the onion becomes translucent. Pour in the wine and simmer for 2 minutes until the liquid reduces a little. Add the chicken to the pan and cover with the chicken stock. Bring to the boil and season with salt and pepper. Simmer for 1 hour, then turn off the heat and leave the chicken to steep in the stock for 30 minutes. Remove the chicken from the pan and allow to cool for 30 minutes.

For the pistou, place all the ingredients in a blender and mix until combined.

Strip the chicken meat from the bones and cut into small pieces, then return it to the soup with the baby beans and asparagus. Stir in the chervil, parsley and tarragon and cook for a further 3 minutes. Season with salt and pepper.

Pour the soup into bowls, then mix through a little of the pistou at the last minute. Serve with some crusty bread.

SERVES 4

Eggplant parmigiana

This is my version of Italy's most famous eggplant dish – melanzane alla parmigiana. I like to take it straight from the oven to the table in a large earthenware dish for everyone to share. Bellissimo!

150 ml extra virgin olive oil
5 golden shallots, peeled
  and finely chopped
3 cloves garlic, crushed
50 ml white wine vinegar
1.5 kg vine-ripened tomatoes
100 g tomato paste
salt and pepper
½ bunch oregano, leaves
  picked and chopped
2 medium eggplants (aubergines),
  cut into 1 cm thick slices
200 g parmesan (preferably
  reggiano), grated

Preheat the oven to 180°C.

Heat 50 ml olive oil in a frying pan and cook the shallots and garlic until soft. Pour in the white wine vinegar and simmer until the liquid has evaporated. Remove the seeds from half of the tomatoes, roughly chop the flesh and add to the shallots. Stir in the tomato paste and season with salt and pepper. Cook over low heat for 15 minutes, then add the chopped oregano and check the seasoning.

Sprinkle the eggplant slices with a little salt and leave for 10 minutes to remove the bitter juices. Pat the slices dry with a cloth. Heat the remaining olive oil in a large frying pan, add the eggplant and fry on both sides until golden brown. Drain the eggplant on kitchen paper to remove the excess oil.

Cut the remaining tomatoes into 5 mm thick slices.

Spoon some sauce over the base of individual gratin dishes or a large earthenware dish. Add layers of sliced tomato, eggplant and oregano until everything is used up, finishing with a layer of sauce. Top with the grated parmesan and bake for 15–20 minutes until the cheese is golden brown.

SERVES 4

Preserved artichokes

Every winter, when globe artichokes are in season, I buy a few boxes to preserve – in this recipe, they are essentially pickled in wine and vinegar. Serve just as they are with a little melted butter (as below), or add them to salads, pasta dishes or antipasto platters. To prepare the preserving jars, place them in boiling water for 2 minutes, then leave to drip dry. Fill the jars with the hot artichokes and cooking liquid to within 1 cm of the top. Allow to cool, then seal tightly and store in the fridge for up to 2 months.

3 kg globe artichokes
50 ml lemon juice
200 ml extra virgin olive oil
1 brown onion, sliced
4 quarters preserved lemon,
   rind only
4 cloves garlic, finely chopped
salt and pepper
100 ml white wine
350 ml white wine vinegar
melted butter, to serve
chopped flat-leaf parsley, to serve

Remove the outer leaves of the artichokes and shave away the green skin from the stem. Toss the artichokes with some lemon juice to prevent browning and cut each one into six to eight pieces.

Heat the olive oil in a frying pan, add the onion, preserved lemon and garlic and cook for 3–4 minutes or until the onion is tender. Season with salt and pepper, then pour in the white wine and vinegar and bring to the boil. Add the artichokes and simmer for about 30 minutes until tender. Remove from the heat and allow to cool. Serve with melted butter and chopped parsley.

SERVES 6

Veal osso bucco with soft polenta

Like many peasant-style dishes, osso bucco requires long, slow simmering to let it shine. The marrow in the bone gradually cooks into the braising liquid to give the sauce its rich, unique flavour. Traditionally, osso bucco is served with risotto Milanese, but I prefer it with soft polenta.

1.2 kg veal osso bucco
salt and pepper
olive oil, for pan-frying
1 carrot, chopped
1 leek, chopped
1 celery stalk, chopped
6 cloves garlic, chopped
2 thyme sprigs
6 vine-ripened tomatoes,
    seeded and chopped
100 ml Madeira
2 litres chicken stock
grated zest of 1 orange
grated zest of 1 lemon
1 bay leaf
10 g butter
½ carrot, extra, finely diced
½ leek, extra, finely chopped
¼ celeriac, finely diced
1 tablespoon chopped
    flat-leaf parsley
2 vine-ripened tomatoes,
    extra, seeded and diced

Gremolata
½ bunch flat-leaf parsley
½ clove garlic
100 ml olive oil
60 ml lemon juice
salt and pepper

Polenta
150 g polenta
40 g butter
40 g parmesan (preferably
    reggiano), grated
1 tablespoon crème fraîche
salt and pepper

Season the osso bucco with salt and pepper. Heat a little oil in a large saucepan, add the osso bucco and sear both sides until golden. Remove from the pan.

Add the carrot, leek, celery, garlic and thyme to the pan and cook for 3–4 minutes until lightly brown. Add the chopped tomatoes and Madeira and simmer until reduced by a third. Return the osso bucco to the pan and cover with the chicken stock, citrus zest and bay leaf. Season with salt and pepper, then cover and braise over medium heat for 2–3 hours until the meat is tender.

Meanwhile, prepare the gremolata. Pick the leaves from the parsley, then use the pulse setting on a blender to mix the parsley, garlic and olive oil until combined. You could also do this in a mortar and pestle. Add lemon juice to taste and season with salt and pepper.

To prepare the polenta, bring 750 ml water to the boil in a saucepan. Sprinkle in the polenta and cook for 15 minutes, stirring constantly, then stir in the butter, grated parmesan and crème fraiche. Season with salt and pepper to taste.

Remove the osso bucco from the liquid. Cover and keep warm. Strain the cooking juices and return to the pan, skimming off any excess oil, then simmer until reduced to your desired consistency.

Melt the butter in a separate saucepan and cook the extra carrot, extra leek and the celeriac for 2–3 minutes until the leek starts to become translucent. Add this mixture to the sauce, then stir in the parsley and extra diced tomato.

To serve, spoon the polenta onto a plate. Arrange the meat and vegetables on the polenta and spoon the sauce over the top. Finish with a spoonful of gremolata and serve.

SERVES 6

French onion soup with gruyère croutons

Patience is its own reward with this classic soup, as the sliced onions have to slowly cook for 90 minutes until they are golden brown. Make sure they are cooked over low heat to prevent them from burning, as the bitter, burnt flavour would be imparted to the whole soup.

250 g butter
10 brown onions, sliced
10 cloves garlic, sliced
1 thyme sprig
1 bay leaf
100 ml Madeira
70 g plain flour
1.5 litres chicken stock
salt and pepper
1 small baguette
60 g gruyère

In a medium saucepan, combine the butter, onion, garlic, thyme and bay leaf and cook over low heat, stirring occasionally, for 1½ hours or until golden brown. Add the Madeira and simmer until the liquid has reduced to a syrup. Stir in the flour and cook for 5 minutes.

Bring the chicken stock to the boil. Add to the pan, season the soup with salt and pepper and cook for a further 20 minutes.

Slice the bread into 4 mm thick pieces and toast lightly under the grill. Grate the gruyère onto the bread and return to the grill until it has melted.

Pour the soup into bowls and serve with the gruyère croutons.

SERVES 6

Chilli salt mud crab with lime and coriander

Question: *Why don't chefs like to share their plate of mud crab?* **Answer:** *Because they're shellfish!* OK, OK, the joke was funnier when my son Harry told it, but at the same time it is quite accurate, as anyone who has seen me gnawing away on a crab claw in Chinatown will know. This recipe is tried and true, and the tempura flour (which is available from Asian supermarkets) gives the crab a thin, crisp and salty coating. Just add limes and a very large bib!

1 × 2 kg mud crab
1 egg white
vegetable oil, for deep-frying
1 long red chilli, sliced
coriander leaves, to garnish
2 limes, cut in half

Chilli salt mix
40 g onion powder
40 g garlic powder
10 g chilli powder
10 g black pepper
25 g salt
180 g tempura flour

Bring a large saucepan of salted water to the boil, then cook the mud crab for 4–5 minutes. Remove the crab, drain and allow to cool.

Prepare the chilli salt mix by combining all of the ingredients.

Remove the top outer shell of the crab and clean under water. Remove the gill from the crab, then the two claws and lightly crack with the back of a knife. Cut the crab body in half. Brush the crab pieces with the egg white. Toss the crab shells through the chilli salt mix and shake off any excess.

Half-fill a deep-fryer or heavy-based saucepan with oil and heat to 200°C (a cube of bread dropped in the oil should brown in 10 seconds). Add the crab pieces and cook for 2–3 minutes or until crisp and golden. Remove and drain on kitchen paper.

To serve, place the crab pieces on a platter and garnish with the sliced chilli, coriander and lime halves.

SERVES 4

Goat's cheese ravioli with broccolini, zucchini and muscatels

Who can resist the combination of acidic goat's cheese, sweet muscatels, golden pine nuts and nut-brown butter? I regularly serve this at home as a main course with a crunchy salad of witlof and cos lettuce on the side.

2 bunches broccolini,
   cut into florets
2 zucchini (courgettes),
   sliced into ribbons with
   a vegetable peeler
200 g butter
2 lemons, segmented
2 tablespoons muscatels
50 g pine nuts, toasted

Pasta
250 g pasta flour
5 egg yolks
1 egg
1 teaspoon extra virgin olive oil
1 teaspoon salt

Goat's cheese filling
500 g soft goat's cheese
¼ bunch mint, leaves picked
   and chopped
60 g pine nuts, toasted
salt and pepper

To prepare the pasta, place all the ingredients in a food processor and blend to a breadcrumb consistency. Tip out onto a lightly floured bench and knead until smooth. Wrap in plastic film and rest for 20 minutes.

To make the filling, combine the goat's cheese, mint and pine nuts in a large bowl and season to taste with salt and pepper. Divide the mixture into 18 balls.

To make the ravioli, roll out the pasta in a pasta machine until very thin. Cut the pasta sheet in half and lightly brush one sheet with water. Place the goat's cheese balls on the moistened pasta sheet, leaving about 2 cm between each one. Lay the second pasta sheet on top. Mould the pasta over and around the filling, trying to remove as much air as possible, then cut out the ravioli with a 5 cm circular cutter.

Blanch the ravioli in a large saucepan of salted boiling water for 2 minutes, then remove with a slotted spoon, drain and arrange on warm plates.

Add the broccolini to the boiling water and blanch for 1½ minutes. Add the zucchini ribbons and cook for a further 10 seconds. Drain the vegetables and arrange over the ravioli.

To serve, heat the butter in a saucepan until it foams and turns a light golden-brown colour. Add the lemon segments, muscatels and toasted pine nuts, toss to coat, then spoon over the ravioli.

SERVES 6

Tempura soft-shell crab with aïoli

You can now buy fresh soft-shell crab in Australia as they are farmed in far-north Queensland. This recipe is a simple way to serve them. If you want to serve it as a main course, it is terrific with an Asian-style salad of mint, lime, bamboo shoots, cucumber, chilli and peanuts.

vegetable oil, for deep-frying
500 g soft-shell crabs,
   cut in half
salt and pepper
2 lemons

Tempura batter
100 g plain flour
50 g cornflour
25 g baking powder
250 ml iced water
1 teaspoon salt

Quick aïoli
100 g mayonnaise
½ clove garlic, crushed
juice of ½ lemon
salt and pepper

To make the aïoli, mix together the mayonnaise, garlic and lemon juice and season with salt and pepper. Cover and leave to infuse in the refrigerator for at least an hour, then remove from the fridge and pass through a fine sieve.

To prepare the tempura batter, place all the ingredients in a bowl and whisk to a thin batter consistency.

Half-fill a deep-fryer or heavy-based frying pan with oil and heat to 180°C (a cube of bread dropped in the oil should brown in 15 seconds).

Pat the crab pieces dry, then pass them through the batter and carefully lower into the hot oil. Cook for about 2 minutes until golden brown, then remove and drain on kitchen paper. Season with salt and pepper, then serve immediately with lemon cheeks and some aïoli on the side.

SERVES 4

barbecues, salads & picnics

Lamb marinated in yoghurt

This is my take on a lamb kebab. Ras el hanout is a spice mix often used in north African and Middle Eastern cooking, particularly with beef, lamb or poultry or stirred into couscous or rice. Store the leftovers in an airtight container for up to 3 months. If you are short of time, you can always buy the spice mix from gourmet food stores and spice shops.

100 g yoghurt

1 teaspoon ras el hanout
(see below)

¼ bunch mint, leaves picked
and roughly chopped

600 g lamb backstrap,
sinew removed

salt and pepper

2 teaspoons extra virgin olive oil

1 preserved lemon rind,
rinsed and thinly sliced

roast capsicum (pepper), to serve

grilled eggplant (aubergine),
to serve

rocket, to serve

Ras el hanout

1 tablespoon ground cumin

1 tablespoon ground ginger

1 tablespoon table salt

3 teaspoons freshly ground
black pepper

2 teaspoons ground cinnamon

2 teaspoons ground coriander

2 teaspoons cayenne pepper

1 teaspoon ground cloves

2 teaspoons ground fennel seeds

To prepare the ras el hanout, mix all the ingredients together.

Combine the yoghurt, ras el hanout and half the mint in a large bowl. Add the lamb and coat with the marinade. Cover and leave to marinate for at least 2 hours, preferably overnight.

Preheat the barbecue to its hottest setting or place a chargrill pan over high heat. Season the lamb with a little salt and pepper and drizzle with olive oil and chargrill for 2 minutes each side. Set aside to rest for 5 minutes.

Cut the lamb into slices and arrange on a plate. Scatter the preserved lemon and remaining mint over the top. Serve with roast capsicum, grilled eggplant and rocket leaves.

SERVES 6

Beetroot roasted with fetta and watercress

This is a salad I serve in the cooler autumn months when there is an abundance of beetroot around. I prefer the extra-sweet flavour of baby beetroot but this salad is just as good with larger beetroot. I do suggest that you use rubber gloves to peel the beetroot or your hands will be stained red for days afterwards! I love to use Persian fetta from the Yarra Valley, but you could just as easily use Bulgarian or Hungarian fetta.

10 small beetroots
sea salt and pepper
100 ml white wine vinegar
100 ml extra virgin olive oil
100 g Persian fetta or any other
   soft, marinated fetta
½ bunch watercress
50 ml balsamic vinegar

Preheat the oven to 180°C.

Spread a large piece of foil on the kitchen bench and place the beetroots on top. Season with salt and pepper, then bring the edges of the foil together. Pour the white wine vinegar over the beetroots and secure the edges to make a bag. Place the bag on a baking tray in case of any spillage. Cook in the oven for 20 minutes until tender, then remove and allow to cool. Using rubber gloves, peel the beetroots and cut them in half.

Heat 20 ml extra virgin olive oil in a saucepan, add the beetroot and cook for a few minutes to sear slightly. Season to taste. Transfer the beetroot to a serving dish and crumble the fetta over the top.

Arrange the watercress around the beetroot. Whisk together the balsamic vinegar and remaining olive oil and drizzle over the salad before serving.

SERVES 4

Smoked salmon rillettes

The term 'rillettes' traditionally refers to pork that has been cooked slowly in fat and shredded to form a paste similar to pâté. In this recipe, I have used a combination of smoked and poached salmon with capers and horseradish. Serve it on slices of toasted bread as a pre-dinner nibble, or for lunch with a fresh baguette, a green salad and a chilled bottle of rosé.

1 litre vegetable stock
salt
300 g salmon fillet
150 g smoked salmon, chopped
100 ml crème fraîche
½ bunch dill, chopped
½ bunch chives, chopped
pinch cayenne pepper
grated zest of 1 lemon
1 teaspoon grated horseradish
2 teaspoons capers, rinsed

Bring the stock to the boil and season to taste with salt. Place the salmon fillet in a heatproof bowl, then pour over enough boiling stock to cover. Cover the bowl with plastic film and set aside to poach for 30 minutes. Remove the salmon from the stock and remove any skin.

Place the remaining ingredients in a bowl and mix until all combined.

Flake the poached salmon and gently fold into the crème fraîche mixture. Season with salt and a little more cayenne pepper if desired. Spoon the smoked salmon rillettes into jars and store in the fridge for up to 4 days.

SERVES 6

Grilled quail with grapes and bitter lettuce

I love the sweet and sour flavours of this dish, stemming from the honey and verjuice. It is important to let the quail rest after cooking otherwise the meat will not be as tender as it should be.

500 g quail breasts
salt and pepper
olive oil, for rubbing
5 teaspoons honey
75 ml verjuice
100 g black grapes,
    cut in half
50 g butter
2 radicchio lettuce,
    leaves washed and torn
¼ bunch flat-leaf parsley,
    leaves picked

Season the quail breasts with salt and pepper and rub with a little olive oil. Place the quail, skin-side down, on a chargrill plate over medium–high heat and cook for a couple of minutes. Turn the breasts over and cook for a further minute. Remove from the chargrill and leave to rest for about 10 minutes.

In a small saucepan, bring the honey to the boil and cook for 2 minutes until the colour begins to darken. Stir in the verjuice and grapes. Just prior to serving, stir in the butter, a little at a time.

To serve, arrange the radicchio and parsley leaves on a plate. Lay the quail breasts on the leaves and spoon the sauce and grapes over the top.

SERVES 6

Salad of tomato, capers, red onion and preserved lemon

The key to this salad is to use the best tomatoes you can lay your hands on – vine-ripened are ideal, but if you can't find them use ruby-red egg tomatoes. I also prefer to use the baby Sicilian or Spanish capers in salt as they have a more delicate flavour than the larger capers in brine.

4 vine-ripened tomatoes,
    cut into 4 mm thick slices
½ small red onion, finely sliced
2 teaspoons baby capers, rinsed
¼ preserved lemon, rind only,
    thinly sliced
salt and pepper
3 large basil leaves, cut into
    thin strips

Dressing
40 ml extra virgin olive oil
20 ml aged balsamic vinegar

To make the dressing, whisk together the oil and vinegar until combined.

Arrange the tomato slices on a serving plate, followed by a layer of finely sliced onion and a scattering of baby capers and preserved lemon. Drizzle the dressing over the salad and season with salt and pepper. Sprinkle with the chopped basil just before serving.

SERVES 6

Lamb kofta

This recipe was born out of the first series of *The Chopping Block*, when we were trying to breathe life into the menu of a faltering Egyptian restaurant. It's a great lunch dish for summer, served with a Greek salad and fresh pita bread. If you are using bamboo skewers, make sure you soak them in water for about an hour beforehand, so they don't scorch during cooking. Japanese panko breadcrumbs are available from most supermarkets.

1 cinnamon quill
2 teaspoons coriander seeds
2 teaspoons cumin seeds
1 teaspoon ground ginger
2 teaspoons salt
50 ml olive oil
1 brown onion, finely diced
3 cloves garlic, finely sliced
600 g minced lean lamb
¼ bunch flat-leaf parsley, leaves
    picked and finely chopped
50 g pine nuts, toasted
50 g fresh or Japanese panko
    breadcrumbs
lemon cheeks, to serve
6 tablespoons tahini

Place the cinnamon quill, coriander, cumin, ginger and salt in a frying pan and heat gently until the seeds start to pop and release their flavour. Transfer the spices to a mortar and pestle and grind to a fine powder.

Heat a little olive oil in a small saucepan over low heat and sauté the onion and garlic for about 10 minutes until slightly translucent. Stir in the spice powder and cook for a further 5 minutes. Remove from the heat and allow to cool.

Place the minced lamb in a bowl, add the spiced onion and garlic mixture, parsley, pine nuts and breadcrumbs and mix together well. Divide the mixture into six portions and mould each portion around a skewer.

Preheat the barbecue to its hottest setting or place a chargrill pan over high heat. Add the lamb skewers and cook for 10 minutes, turning every couple of minutes to ensure they cook evenly. Place the skewers on a platter and serve with lemon cheeks and tahini.

SERVES 6

Caesar salad

This is my take on a Caesar salad without any bacon or pancetta in it. I like to serve the poached egg warm straight from the pan so that when you cut into it, the yolk mixes with the Caesar dressing to coat the lettuce. I suggest using a neutral-flavoured oil such as grapeseed for this dressing, as olive oil has a dominant flavour that can be overwhelming here.

½ loaf ciabatta
20 ml olive oil
salt and pepper
1 teaspoon salt
50 ml white wine vinegar
4 eggs
4 baby cos lettuce
50 g parmesan (preferably reggiano), shaved
8 pickled white anchovies

Caesar dressing
2 egg yolks
3 teaspoons Dijon mustard
20 ml lemon juice
1 clove garlic, roughly chopped
4 anchovy fillets
salt and pepper
150 ml grapeseed oil
1 tablespoon finely grated parmesan (preferably reggiano)

Preheat the oven to 180°C.

To prepare the Caesar dressing, purée the egg yolks, mustard, lemon juice, garlic, anchovy fillets, salt and pepper in a blender, then with the motor running, slowly add the oil until completely incorporated. Pour the mixture into a bowl and fold in the grated parmesan. If the dressing is too thick, thin it down with a little water.

Roughly cut the ciabatta into 1 cm cubes and toss them in the olive oil. Season with salt and pepper, then place on a baking tray and bake for 5 minutes or until golden brown and crunchy.

To poach the eggs, half-fill a large saucepan with water, stir in the salt and white wine vinegar and bring to the boil. Reduce the heat so the water is just simmering, then carefully crack the eggs into the water and poach gently until the white starts to set (this should take about 2–3 minutes).

Meanwhile, wash the baby cos leaves and place in a large bowl. Dress with about two-thirds of the dressing.

To serve, arrange the leaves in four bowls and scatter with the croûtons, shaved parmesan and anchovies. Remove the eggs from the water and drain them on kitchen paper. Place the eggs in the centre of the salads and drizzle with the remaining dressing. Serve immediately.

SERVES 4

Warm salad of grilled field mushrooms This dish

is a great vegetarian starter to serve in autumn, or serve it as a side dish with Confit of duck with green beans (see page 134).

320 g field mushrooms,
    peeled and trimmed
2 thyme sprigs, leaves picked
2 cloves garlic, crushed
50 ml olive oil
salt and pepper
1 handful rocket

Red wine vinaigrette
30 ml red wine vinegar
1 teaspoon Dijon mustard
1 teaspoon seeded mustard
salt and pepper
60 ml olive oil

Toss the mushrooms, thyme and garlic in the olive oil. Season to taste, then cover and marinate in the refrigerator for at least an hour, preferably overnight.

To prepare the vinaigrette, whisk together the vinegar and mustards and season with salt and pepper. Whisking constantly, slowly pour in the olive oil until combined.

Preheat the barbecue to its hottest setting or place a chargrill pan over high heat. Remove the mushrooms from the oil and chargrill for about 2 minutes, then turn over and cook for a further 1–2 minutes.

Arrange the mushrooms and rocket on a plate, drizzle with the red wine vinaigrette and serve.

SERVES 6

Shaved fennel, bitter lettuce, figs and blue cheese

This salad is ideal to serve in late summer or early autumn when figs, fennel and radicchio are at their best. Make sure you hang on to the fennel fronds as they add a fresh aniseed flavour to the salad.

2 baby fennel, trimmed and
  thinly shaved, fronds reserved
2 radicchio lettuce, washed
  and leaves picked
100 g roquefort or gorgonzola
  picante
6 figs, cut into quarters

Vinaigrette
2 teaspoons white wine vinegar
2 teaspoons champagne vinegar
1 teaspoon lemon juice
1 teaspoon Dijon mustard
salt and pepper
80 ml grapeseed oil

To prepare the vinaigrette, whisk together the vinegars, lemon juice and mustard and season with salt and pepper. Whisking constantly, slowly pour in the grapeseed oil until combined.

Place the fennel and radicchio leaves in a bowl. Drizzle with the vinaigrette and toss until all the leaves are dressed.

Arrange the salad on a serving plate and crumble the cheese over the top. Place the fig quarters on top, sprinkle with the reserved fennel fronds and serve.

SERVES 6

Barbecue chicken with chermoula rub

This is a great summer dish – you can fire up the barbecue while the chicken is marinating. Spoon any extra chermoula into a jar and top with a layer of olive oil. It will keep for 3 or 4 days, and can be used to marinate lamb chops or firm-textured fish such as hapuka.

1 × 1.6 kg chicken, cut in half
  and flattened
1 lemon, cut into quarters

Chermoula rub
½ bunch coriander, chopped
½ bunch flat-leaf parsley,
  leaves picked and chopped
3 cloves garlic, chopped
1 tablespoon chopped ginger
¾ teaspoon sweet paprika
¾ teaspoon cumin seeds,
  roasted and ground
¾ teaspoon coriander seeds,
  roasted and ground
150 ml extra virgin olive oil
juice of ¾ lemon
¾ long red chilli, finely chopped
1 teaspoon salt

To prepare the chermoula rub, mix all the ingredients together until combined. Massage the marinade all over the chicken and leave to marinate for at least an hour.

Preheat the barbecue to its hottest setting or place a chargrill pan over high heat.

Cook the chicken, skin-side down, for 10 minutes, then turn it over and cook for a further 10 minutes or until cooked through (check by inserting a skewer into the leg – the chicken is cooked if the skewer is warm to touch when removed). Transfer the chicken to a plate and serve with lemon wedges.

SERVES 4

Salad of beetroot, goat's cheese and lettuce with hazelnut dressing

This beetroot salad is a good one to serve in summer when there are plenty of baby salad green leaves available. Soignon buche blanche goat's cheese adds a rich flavour with echoes of nuts and mushrooms. You could also use any other local white-mould goat's cheese, such as Holy Goat from South Australia or Jannei from the Blue Mountains in New South Wales. The salad lends itself to many different types of lettuce – I sometimes use rocket or mixed baby cos leaves as an alternative, mixed with some freshly torn basil.

20 ml white wine vinegar,
    plus an extra splash
1 teaspoon honey
1 teaspoon Dijon mustard
60 ml hazelnut oil
salt and pepper
18 baby beetroots, trimmed
    and scrubbed
½ bunch baby chard
1 tray mache lettuce
½ punnet mizuna lettuce
180 g log Soignon buche blanche
    goat's cheese or other white-
    mould goat's cheese, cut into
    1.5 cm slices
60 g hazelnuts, roasted

Whisk together the white wine vinegar, honey and mustard. Continue to whisk while slowly drizzling in the hazelnut oil until combined. Season to taste with salt and pepper.

Place the baby beetroots in a saucepan and cover with cold water. Add a splash of white wine vinegar and a teaspoon of salt. Bring to the boil, then reduce the heat and simmer for about 20 minutes until the beets are tender. Drain and leave to cool. Once cool, peel away the skins and cut the beetroots into quarters.

Assemble the salad leaves on a plate and arrange the beetroot and goat's cheese on top. Spoon on the hazelnut dressing and roasted hazelnuts and serve.

SERVES 6

Marinated octopus

I love the charred flavour of grilled octopus but I prefer to braise it first to tenderise it and add flavour. Try serving it as part of a tapas plate with tzatziki, Spanish gordal olives and a crisp, dry white wine.

500 g octopus tentacles
3 red chillies, finely chopped
4 cloves garlic, finely chopped
¼ bunch parsley, leaves picked
    and finely chopped
100 ml extra virgin olive oil,
    plus extra for chargrilling
salt and pepper
200 ml white wine
50 ml chardonnay vinegar
½ bunch rocket

Rinse the octopus tentacles and pat dry with kitchen paper. Cut the tentacles into 5 cm pieces and place in a bowl with the chilli, garlic, parsley and olive oil. Season to taste, then cover with plastic film and marinate in the refrigerator for 1 hour.

Transfer the marinated octopus to a heavy-based saucepan and cook over high heat for 2 minutes. Add the white wine and chardonnay vinegar, then cover and simmer for 5–10 minutes or until the octopus is tender. Drain off the liquid.

Toss the octopus in a little olive oil, then chargrill for 2 minutes or until lightly charred. Serve immediately on a bed of rocket.

SERVES 6

Salad of witlof, apples and walnuts with a honey mustard dressing

The honey and mustard dressing makes a lovely contrast to the slight bitterness of the witlof in this salad. For a relaxed Sunday brunch, serve it with Smoked trout and asparagus tart (see page 120).

1 red witlof, washed and
  leaves picked
1 white witlof, washed
  and leaves picked
2 handfuls rocket
1 green apple, sliced
70 g walnuts, roasted

Honey and mustard dressing
20 ml white wine vinegar
1 teaspoon Dijon mustard
1 teaspoon seeded mustard
2 teaspoons honey
70 ml grapeseed oil
salt and pepper

To make the dressing, whisk together the vinegar, mustards and honey, then slowly whisk in the oil until combined. Season to taste with salt and pepper.

Place the witlof leaves, rocket and apple in a bowl. Drizzle the dressing over the top and toss until all the leaves are dressed. Scatter with the roasted walnuts and serve.

SERVES 6

Panzanella

Panzanella is a classic Italian bread salad, but my version is slightly different. I try and use three or four different varieties of tomatoes in season to add colour and flavour. This is such a substantial dish that I generally serve it as a starter rather than a side salad.

¼ loaf white sourdough bread
2 vine-ripened tomatoes,
    cut into wedges
1 punnet yellow cherry tomatoes,
    cut in half
1 punnet red cherry tomatoes,
    cut in half
½ red onion, cut into 1 cm dice
1 large cucumber, seeded and
    cut into 1 cm dice
5–6 basil leaves, torn
40 ml red wine vinegar
80 ml extra virgin olive oil
salt and pepper

Preheat the oven to 160°C.

Tear the sourdough into bite-sized chunks, place on a baking tray and bake for about 10 minutes until golden and crunchy. Remove from the oven and allow to cool.

Combine the tomatoes, onion, cucumber and basil in a large bowl. Whisk together the red wine vinegar and olive oil, pour over the salad and toss gently to coat. Season with salt and pepper. Add the cooled sourdough pieces, toss again and serve.

SERVES 6

Barbecue steaks with chimichurri sauce

Sirloin is a very versatile cut of meat and has more flavour than fillet. Chimichurri sauce is a vibrant green Argentinean sauce made with fresh herbs. It makes a great accompaniment for the sirloin, and also works well with lamb or chicken. I use garlic confit in this recipe for its soft, mellow flavour. Bake the cloves in their skins in an ovenproof dish of extra virgin olive oil for approximately 20 minutes at 150°C until they are soft.

6 × 200 g sirloin steaks
salt and pepper
extra virgin olive oil, for brushing

Chimichurri sauce
¼ bunch coriander, leaves picked
½ bunch basil, leaves picked
½ bunch flat-leaf parsley,
   leaves picked
1 teaspoon ground cumin
5 cloves garlic confit (see above)
1 golden shallot, peeled
300 ml olive oil
2 teaspoons red wine vinegar

To make the chimichurri sauce, place the herbs, cumin, garlic confit, golden shallot and olive oil in a food processor and blend until combined. Add the red wine vinegar just prior to serving.

Preheat the barbecue to its hottest setting or place a chargrill pan over high heat.

Season the steaks with salt and pepper and brush with a little olive oil, then grill for about 3 minutes on each side, turning only once. Remove the steaks, cover loosely with foil and rest for 10 minutes.

Slice the steaks and serve with the chimichurri sauce.

SERVES 6

Haloumi with watermelon and mint

A friend of mine from Cyprus tells me he grew up eating large wedges of watermelon with chunks of salty, chewy haloumi. While it may sound like an unusual combination, the sweetness of the watermelon is the ideal foil for the piquant flavour of the cheese. If you like, the saltiness of the haloumi can be reduced by soaking it in cold water for 20 minutes before using.

2 teaspoons vegetable oil
500 g haloumi, cut
    into 1 cm slices
1 kg watermelon, peeled
    and cut into chunks
¼ bunch mint
20 ml extra virgin olive oil
1 lemon, cut in half

Heat the vegetable oil in a non-stick frying pan and cook the haloumi on both sides for about 2 minutes until golden brown.

Arrange the watermelon on a plate with the hot haloumi cheese. Pick the mint leaves and scatter over the top. Drizzle the olive oil over the salad and finish with a squeeze of lemon juice.

SERVES 6

Peach, prosciutto and mozzarella salad

My family and I live on this salad in summer. We sometimes eat it as a starter or make a large one for the table and have it with Fried school prawns with aïoli (see page 50). For the best flavour, you must use really ripe peaches (the slipstone variety are a good choice) – later in the year you could use white peaches or plums.

20 ml extra virgin olive oil
20 ml balsamic vinegar
salt and pepper
2 ripe yellow peaches
1 handful rocket
¼ bunch mint, leaves picked
2 buffalo mozzarella balls,
　cut into 12 pieces
4 slices prosciutto,
　torn into pieces

Whisk together the olive oil and balsamic vinegar and season with salt and pepper.

Blanch the peaches in a pan of boiling water for 10 seconds, then remove. When cool enough to handle, peel off the skin and cut each peach into eight slices.

Dress the rocket and mint with the balsamic dressing and arrange on a plate. Place the peaches and mozzarella on top, then lay the prosciutto over the salad and serve.

SERVES 4

Iceberg, egg, pea and fetta salad

This salad is a great combination of salty fetta, sweet hazelnut dressing, fresh mint and the crisp crunch of chilled iceberg lettuce. An excellent crowd pleaser to serve in the summer.

2 eggs
1 iceberg lettuce
100 g shelled peas
100 g Persian fetta or any other
   soft, marinated fetta
¼ bunch mint, leaves picked
1 red onion, finely sliced

Hazelnut dressing
3 teaspoons hazelnut oil
3 teaspoons olive oil
3 teaspoons balsamic vinegar
salt and pepper

To make the dressing, whisk together the oils and vinegar and season to taste.

Add the eggs to a saucepan of boiling water and boil for 3½ minutes. Remove the eggs from the pan and run under cold water to stop the cooking process. When cool, peel and cut into quarters.

Cut the iceberg into eight wedges and wash under running water to remove any debris.

Blanch the peas in boiling water for 30 seconds. Drain, then refresh in iced water to maintain their colour.

Arrange the lettuce on a plate and add the crumbled fetta, eggs, peas, mint and red onion. Drizzle the hazelnut dressing over the salad and serve.

SERVES 6

Grilled tuna with capsicum and olives

I use the barbecue a lot in summer because I love the smoky, charred flavour it gives food. Make sure you don't overcook the tuna as it will be dry and unappetising if left on the grill for too long. Any extra piperade can be used the next day, folded through an omelette or frittata.

80 g small olives, pitted
½ bunch basil, leaves picked
6 × 180 g tuna fillets

Piperade
3 red capsicums (peppers)
3 yellow capsicums (peppers)
100 ml olive oil
1 rosemary sprig
2 red onions, thinly sliced
150 ml red wine vinegar
salt and pepper

To prepare the piperade, roast the capsicums over a naked flame until they are black. Place in a bowl, cover with plastic film and leave to steam for about 10 minutes. Peel off the blackened skin and cut the flesh into thin strips.

Heat the olive oil and rosemary in a saucepan, add the onion and cook until translucent. Stir in the red wine vinegar and simmer for 4–5 minutes until the liquid has almost disappeared. Add the capsicum strips and season to taste.

Shortly before you are ready to serve, stir the olives and basil through the piperade and allow to warm through.

Preheat the barbecue to its hottest setting or place a chargrill pan over high heat. Chargrill the tuna fillets for 1 minute each side until medium–rare.

Spoon some piperade onto the centre of each plate, place a tuna fillet on top and serve.

SERVES 6

Smoked trout and asparagus tart
I often make this simple tart for a Sunday brunch and serve it with a salad of green leaves and avocado, or whatever I have handy. I know from personal experience that it also makes a very satisfying late-night snack.

1 bunch asparagus, trimmed
3 eggs
200 ml cream
100 ml milk
¼ bunch dill, chopped
salt and pepper
300 g piece hot-smoked
   rainbow trout
50 g parmesan (preferably
   reggiano)

Shortcrust pastry
250 g plain flour
½ teaspoon table salt
pinch castor sugar
160 g butter, slightly softened
1 egg
20 ml milk

To prepare the shortcrust pastry, rub the flour, salt and sugar with the butter until you form a crumb consistency. Mix in the egg and milk and knead gently two or three times. Wrap the pastry in plastic film and rest in the fridge for at least 1 hour. Remove from the fridge and allow the pastry to come back to room temperature before rolling.

Roll out the pastry to a thickness of about 5 mm and line a 25 cm tart tin. Prick the base of the pastry with a fork several times, then return to the fridge for about an hour to rest.

Preheat the oven to 160°C.

Cut out a round piece of baking paper about 5 cm larger in diameter than the tart tin. Line the pastry case with the paper and weigh down with some dried beans or rice. Bake for about 12 minutes, then remove the paper and beans and bake for a further 10 minutes. Brush the inside of the tart case with some beaten egg and return to the oven for 2 minutes (this will prevent the pastry from becoming soggy). Remove from the oven and allow to cool.

Slice each asparagus spear into three pieces. Blanch in boiling salted water for 10–20 seconds, then drain and cool in iced water. When the asparagus is cold, drain off the water.

In a bowl, beat together the eggs, cream, milk, dill, salt and pepper. Remove the skin from the trout and carefully flake the flesh, taking care to remove any bones you find in the process. Scatter the trout and asparagus inside the cooled tart case, then pour on the custard. Finely grate some parmesan over the top and bake for 15 minutes or until the custard is set. Allow the tart to cool for 15 minutes, then remove from the tin and cut into wedges to serve.

SERVES 6

special occasions

Avocado soup with soy-marinated tuna

This delicious cold soup makes a great starter during the summer. The soup has a sharp flavour from the wasabi and lime juice, which contrasts well with the rich flavour of the tuna.

20 g castor sugar
4 large cucumbers, peeled
2 avocados, peeled and
    stones removed
100 g wasabi powder
juice of 3 limes
salt and pepper
200 g sashimi-grade tuna,
    cut into 1 cm cubes
30 ml soy sauce
coriander sprigs, to serve

Combine the sugar with 20 ml water in a small saucepan and stir over low heat until the sugar has completely dissolved. Remove the syrup from the heat and allow to cool.

Cut the cucumbers into small pieces, then process in a blender to the consistency of soup. Pass the mixture through a fine sieve to remove any small lumps. Add the avocado, sugar syrup, wasabi, lime juice and seasoning.

Return the mixture to the blender and process until smooth. Pour the soup into bowls.

To serve, dip the tuna into the soy sauce and place in the soup bowls. Garnish with coriander sprigs.

SERVES 6

Gratin of yabbies with mustard and tarragon

I find it really satisfying to cook the occasional retro-style dish such as this. Yabbies can spoil very quickly so it is crucial that you use only live ones, or yabbies that you have witnessed being freshly boiled, otherwise use another crustacean such as prawn or lobster. Remember that yabbies are freshwater not saltwater so you will need to add a little more salt to the cooking water.

8 baby carrots, peeled
12 asparagus spears,
    peeled and trimmed
100 g shelled peas
butter, for pan-frying
200 g cavolo nero
20 yabbies
40 g butter
450 ml milk
20 g plain flour
1 tablespoon Dijon mustard
1 tablespoon seeded mustard
½ bunch tarragon, torn
100 g parmesan (preferably
    reggiano), finely grated
2 egg yolks

Preheat the oven to 180°C.

Blanch the baby carrots in boiling salted water for 1–2 minutes, then add the asparagus and peas and cook for a further 1–2 minutes. Remove from the heat and refresh in iced water. Cut the carrots and asparagus in half, then divide among four ovenproof dishes (about 15 cm in diameter), followed by the peas.

Heat a teaspoon of butter in a frying pan and cook the cavolo nero for about 2 minutes. Drain, then add to the ovenproof dishes.

Bring a saucepan of salted water to the boil and blanch the yabbies for 30 seconds. Remove from the water and allow to cool for a minute before peeling the meat away from the tails. Arrange the meat from five yabbies in each of the dishes.

Melt the butter in a heavy-based saucepan. Bring the milk to the boil in a separate pan. Add the flour to the melted butter and cook over a low heat, stirring constantly, for about 2 minutes. Remove the pan from the heat and slowly incorporate the hot milk. Bring back to the boil, stirring constantly, then simmer gently for 10 minutes. Pass through a sieve into a clean saucepan. Add the mustards, tarragon and cheese and stir until combined. Remove the pan from the heat before stirring in the egg yolks.

Spoon the sauce over the yabby meat, then tap each dish gently on the bench to help spread the sauce evenly over the ingredients. Bake for 10–15 minutes until the top turns golden brown.

SERVES 4

Ocean trout with roasted leeks and red wine butter sauce

The best time to eat ocean trout is in winter when they fatten up and have a more luscious flavour. The red wine butter sauce, or beurre rouge, partners the fish beautifully, and is also delicious with roast beef fillet or venison medallions.

6 medium leeks, well-washed and
  trimmed
1 clove garlic, crushed
1 thyme sprig
80 g butter
20 ml olive oil
6 × 160 g ocean trout fillets,
  skin removed
360 g Roast confit potatoes
  (see page 158)

Red wine butter sauce
3–4 golden shallots, sliced
1 thyme sprig
1 bay leaf
300 ml red wine vinegar
750 ml red wine
150 ml cream
6 peppercorns, crushed
100 g chilled butter, cubed
salt

Preheat the oven to 180°C.

To prepare the sauce, place the shallots, thyme, bay leaf, red wine vinegar and red wine in a frying pan and simmer for about 20 minutes until the mixture has reduced to a glaze. Pour in the cream and simmer for a further 2–3 minutes. Stir in the crushed peppercorns, then add the butter a few cubes at a time, whisking constantly. Keep the heat low to ensure the mixture does not boil. Season to taste with salt, then remove from the heat and strain through a sieve.

Place the leeks in a baking dish and cover with water. Add the garlic, thyme and half the butter and bake for about 15 minutes until tender. Remove from the oven and cut each leek into thirds.

Heat the olive oil in a large frying pan until hot, then add the fillets with the side that didn't have skin facing down. Cook for about 3 minutes until brown, then carefully turn over and cook for a further 2 minutes. Arrange the cooked leeks in the frying pan and add the remaining butter. Spoon the butter and juices over the fish and leeks to baste, then remove the fish from the pan and allow to rest.

To serve, arrange the leeks on a plate and place the fillets on top. Spoon the sauce over the top and serve with roast confit potatoes.

SERVES 6

Tofu with prosciutto, eggplant, yakumi and sesame ponzu

I love to serve this dish as a starter or as an accompaniment to steamed whole white fish such as snapper or blue-eye trevalla. It is also superb as a vegetarian dish – simply omit the prosciutto.

500 g silken tofu
70 g prosciutto, thinly sliced
1 tablespoon cornflour
vegetable oil, for frying
3 Japanese eggplants (aubergines)

Yakumi salad

¼ bunch spring onions,
    cut into thin strips
¼ leek, white part only,
    well-washed and cut
    into thin strips
2.5 cm knob ginger,
    cut into thin strips
½ red chilli, seeded and
    cut into thin strips
¼ bunch coriander,
    leaves picked

Sesame ponzu

3 teaspoons castor sugar
30 ml lemon juice, strained
30 ml sesame oil
90 ml soy sauce
90 ml rice wine vinegar

Remove the tofu from the packet and drain on a clean cloth for about 1 hour. Using a 4 cm circular cutter, cut out 12 rounds.

Lay the sliced prosciutto out on a board and cut into lengths that will be long enough to wrap around each piece of tofu. Dust a little cornflour onto the prosciutto (to help the tofu stick), then roll the tofu in the prosciutto.

To prepare the yakumi salad, mix together all the ingredients.

To make the sesame ponzu, place the sugar and lemon juice in a bowl and stir until the sugar has dissolved. Add the sesame oil, soy sauce and rice wine vinegar and mix well.

Pour about 2 cm vegetable oil into a deep, heavy-based frying pan and heat until a cube of bread dropped in the oil browns in 15 seconds. Cut the eggplants in half lengthways. Add to the oil, skin-side down, and cook for 2 minutes, then turn over and cook for a further minute. Remove and drain on kitchen paper, then peel away the skin and arrange on serving plates. Keep warm while you cook the tofu.

Roll the prosciutto-wrapped tofu in the remaining cornflour and fry in the hot oil for about 4 minutes or until lightly browned, turning halfway through. Drain on kitchen paper.

To serve, place two pieces of tofu on each plate with the eggplant and pour the sesame ponzu around them. Top with yakumi salad.

SERVES 6

Vichyssoise with jamón

This soup can be served cold or hot but I prefer it served chilled. The best jamón is sourced from black Iberian pigs in Spain and is considered the finest ham in the world. As a substitute you could use good-quality prosciutto.

75 g butter
1 large brown onion, sliced
1 clove garlic, finely chopped
2 leeks, white part only,
   well-washed and sliced
salt and pepper
2 desiree potatoes, thinly sliced
100 ml chicken stock
350 ml cream
1 bunch chives, finely chopped
40 g jamón, cut into thin slices

Melt the butter in a large saucepan over low heat, add the onion, garlic, leek and salt and pepper and cook for 10 minutes until softened. Add the sliced potatoes and chicken stock and bring to the boil. Skim the surface to remove any fat, then simmer for a further 15 minutes. Stir in the cream. Purée the soup until smooth, then pass through a fine sieve. Cover and chill for a couple of hours.

Check the seasoning again when the soup is cold and adjust as required. Stir in the chopped chives. Divide among four bowls, sprinkle with the jamón and serve.

SERVES 4

Confit of duck with green beans

I think winter is the best time to eat duck confit, next to a warm fire, with a crusty baguette and plenty of red wine. I always cook lots of duck legs so that the leftovers can be used in a hearty cassoulet, as a filling for tortellini or ravioli, or shredded and served as rillettes with cornichons and Dijon mustard. Duck fat is available in tins from specialty food stores.

1 bunch thyme, leaves
   picked and chopped
200 g rock salt
6 garlic cloves, crushed
6 duck legs
duck fat, to cover
500 g kipfler potatoes,
   washed and cut into
   1 cm thick rounds
240 g green beans, trimmed
extra virgin olive oil,
   for pan-frying

Mix together the thyme, rock salt and 4 cloves crushed garlic in a bowl. Rub each duck leg with the seasoning, then cover and marinate in the fridge for 4–6 hours.

Preheat the oven to 140°C.

Remove the duck legs from the fridge, wash off the seasoning and pat dry. Place the duck in an ovenproof dish and cover with duck fat. Cover and cook in the oven for 3 hours or until the duck is tender. Remove the duck legs from the fat and put to one side to cool. Reserve the duck fat for another occasion.

Increase the oven temperature to 180°C.

Place the potato slices in a roasting tin with a small amount of duck fat and the remaining garlic. Roast for 40 minutes or until golden.

Blanch the beans in salted boiling water for approximately 2 minutes.

Heat a small amount of oil in a frying pan. Add the duck legs, skin-side down, and cook for 1–2 minutes until the skin is crisp. Serve with the green beans and roast kipfler potatoes.

SERVES 6

Scallops with shaved vegetables

This dish is a favourite of mine for a winter dinner party. I like to use the excellent flash-frozen Canadian scallops, but you could also use fresh Hervey Bay scallops or Tasmanian queen scallops if they are available. Any leftover vinaigrette will keep in the fridge for up to 2 weeks. The truffle dressing will keep in the fridge for about a week and works beautifully with a warm salad of quail, chicken or sweetbreads, or use it to dress roast baby potatoes.

30 ml extra virgin olive oil
24 scallops
knob of butter
salt and pepper
juice of 1 lemon
1–2 small kipfler potatoes, shaved
70 g green beans, split
4 asparagus spears, shaved
4 white asparagus spears, shaved
120 g Preserved artichokes
   (see page 69)

Vinaigrette
1 teaspoon white wine vinegar
1 teaspoon champagne vinegar
½ teaspoon lemon juice
½ teaspoon Dijon mustard
salt and pepper
35 ml grapeseed oil

Truffle dressing
1 egg yolk
1 teaspoon sherry vinegar
1 teaspoon Dijon mustard
salt and pepper
40 ml truffle oil
100 ml grapeseed oil
50 ml water

To prepare the vinaigrette, whisk together the vinegars, lemon juice and mustard, then season with salt and pepper. Whisking constantly, slowly pour in the grapeseed oil until combined.

For the truffle dressing, whisk together the egg yolk, vinegar and mustard, then season with salt and pepper. Whisking constantly, slowly drizzle in the truffle oil and grapeseed oil to make a mayonnaise. Whisk in a little water to thin to your preferred consistency.

Line a tray or large plate with kitchen paper. Heat the olive oil in a large non-stick frying pan. When hot, add the scallops and cook for about 1 minute until golden brown. Add the butter to the pan, then turn the scallops over and cook for a further 30 seconds. Remove the scallops from the pan and place on the prepared tray. Season with salt and pepper and then squeeze a little lemon juice over the top.

Blanch the potatoes, split beans and both types of asparagus in salted boiling water for 30 seconds, then remove and strain through a sieve. Place the blanched vegetables in a bowl with the artichokes and season with salt and pepper. Pour on the vinaigrette and toss through the vegetables.

To serve, divide the vegetables among six plates and arrange four scallops on each. Drizzle with about half the truffle dressing and serve.

SERVES 6

John Dory with shaved fennel and aïoli

I only buy John Dory in winter when the fish are larger and have more flavour than at any other time of the year. This is a very simple dish that you could serve with roast potatoes, braised witlof or a gratin of sweet potato.

2 small fennel bulbs, trimmed and finely sliced (reserve the fronds to garnish)
¼ bunch parsley, leaves picked
50 ml extra virgin olive oil, plus extra for pan-frying
25 ml lemon juice
6 × 150 g John Dory fillets
salt and pepper
15 g butter

Quick aïoli
50 g mayonnaise
½ clove garlic, crushed
juice of ½ lemon
salt and pepper

To prepare the aïoli, mix together the mayonnaise, garlic and lemon juice and season with salt and pepper. Cover and leave to infuse in the refrigerator for at least an hour, then remove from the fridge and pass through a fine sieve.

Combine the fennel and parsley in a bowl and season with salt and pepper. Whisk together the olive oil and lemon juice, then pour over the fennel and parsley. Toss to coat.

Heat a dash of olive oil in a large non-stick frying pan over high heat. Season the John Dory fillets with salt and pepper, then add them to the pan, skin-side down. Cook for about 1 minute until golden brown. Turn the fillets over, then add the butter and cook until it turns nut brown. Cook the fish for a further 30–45 seconds (this may seem short, but John Dory is best slightly undercooked).

Divide the fennel salad among six plates and top with the fish fillets. Drizzle the aïoli over the top, sprinkle with the fennel fronds and serve.

SERVES 6

Baked prawns with white bean and hazelnut salad

This Tuscan-inspired prawn salad is a great dish for the winter months. I love the sweet, fat prawns combined with the nutty flavour of the beans, the salty bacon and the subtle sweetness of the hazelnut dressing.

60 g bacon, cut into strips
extra virgin olive oil, for pan-frying
4 vine-ripened tomatoes
300 g tinned cannellini beans
50 g hazelnuts, roasted and
  skins rubbed off, crushed
½ bunch watercress,
  sprigs picked
salt and pepper
12 raw king prawns, peeled and
  deveined, with tails intact

Hazelnut dressing
1 teaspoon Dijon mustard
2 teaspoons white wine vinegar
1 teaspoon honey
50 ml hazelnut oil
salt and pepper

To prepare the dressing, whisk together the mustard, vinegar and honey, then slowly drizzle in the hazelnut oil, whisking constantly. Season to taste with salt and pepper.

Fry the bacon in a little oil for about 3 minutes until crisp. Remove and drain on kitchen paper.

Blanch the tomatoes in salted boiling water for 10 seconds, then submerge them in iced water for a minute to stop the cooking process. Remove from the water and peel away the skins. Cut the tomatoes into quarters and remove the seeds, then cut into 1 cm dice.

Mix together the bacon, diced tomato, cannellini beans, crushed hazelnuts and watercress. Pour the dressing over the top and toss gently to coat.

Heat a dash of olive oil in a non-stick frying pan. Season the prawns with salt and pepper, then cook for 2–3 minutes, turning occasionally. Remove from the pan.

Divide the salad among six bowls. Arrange two prawns on top of each salad and serve immediately.

SERVES 6

Carpaccio of tuna with king prawns and daikon dressing

This elegant dish is the perfect summer starter. Its success depends on the quality of the tuna – it should be firm to touch and have a tight texture with no separations. Yellowfin tuna should be a crimson red colour, while bluefin should be more of a brick browny red.

360 g sashimi-grade tuna,
    thinly sliced
60 g daikon, cut into
    thin strips
¼ bunch coriander,
    leaves picked, plus
    extra to garnish
12 cooked large king prawns,
    peeled and deveined,
    with tails intact
30 g salmon roe
salt and pepper

Daikon dressing
½ teaspoon sesame oil
50 ml rice wine vinegar
20 ml mirin
25 ml light soy sauce
15 g daikon, grated
½ teaspoon finely
    chopped ginger

To make the dressing, whisk together all the ingredients.

Place the tuna slices between two sheets of plastic film and gently flatten with the handle of a knife. Lay the slices on plates.

Arrange the daikon, coriander and prawns in the middle of the tuna. Drizzle over the dressing, then garnish with the salmon roe and extra coriander. Season to taste with salt and pepper.

SERVES 6

Pork shoulder braised in milk with onions and sage

Ask your butcher to bone and skin the pork shoulder and if you ask nicely, he may even roll and tie it for you! This dish has been cooked for centuries in the Veneto region of Italy and is ideally served with risotto or salad leaves.

20 ml extra virgin olive oil
2 kg pork shoulder, skin and bone removed, rolled and tied
2 teaspoons fennel seeds, crushed
salt and pepper
500 g pickling onions, peeled
10 cloves garlic, peeled
1 bunch sage, leaves picked
300 ml white wine
300 ml milk

Preheat the oven to 130°C.

Heat the olive oil in a large ovenproof saucepan or flameproof casserole dish. Season the pork with the crushed fennel seeds, salt and pepper and sear for 5–6 minutes until brown all over. Remove the pork from the pan. Add the onions, garlic and sage leaves to the pan and cook until the onions are lightly browned. Pour in the wine. Return the pork to the pan, cover with a tight-fitting lid and bake for 2 hours or until the wine has almost evaporated.

Remove the saucepan from the oven. Pour the milk over the pork, then return to the oven and bake uncovered for a further 30–40 minutes. When ready, the milk will have thickened and curdled. Spoon this over the pork before serving.

SERVES 6

Melon and prosciutto soup

Melon and prosciutto are a staple on most Italian antipasto plates, and it is these flavours that inspired this chilled soup. Simple to prepare, it is great to serve in the hotter months.

1 small ripe rockmelon
juice of 1 lemon, strained
1 teaspoon salt
½ teaspoon black peppercorns,
    crushed
100 ml extra virgin olive oil
sugar, to taste
12 thin slices baguette
6 slices prosciutto

Remove the skin and seeds from the melon. Cut the melon into small chunks and place in a bowl with the lemon juice, salt, pepper and 80 ml olive oil. Mix with a large spoon, then leave to marinate for about an hour.

Blend the melon mixture until smooth, then pass through a sieve and season with a little sugar if required. Cover and chill for a couple of hours before serving.

Drizzle each side of the bread slices with the remaining olive oil, then chargrill or cook under a hot grill until golden brown.

Pour the soup into six bowls. Place each slice of prosciutto between two slices of bread and serve alongside the soup.

SERVES 6

Coq au vin

This is my version of the classic French chicken dish, something I really enjoy cooking when it is cold and miserable outside. It's not a dish that you can rush, but it is well worth the wait as it nourishes both body and soul.

6 chicken marylands
1.5 litres shiraz or other red wine
1 carrot, roughly chopped
1 celery stalk, roughly chopped
1 onion, roughly chopped
1 clove garlic, finely chopped
1 leek, well-washed and
    roughly chopped
salt and pepper
vegetable oil, for pan-frying
2 litres chicken stock

Coq au vin garnish
12 brown pickling onions, trimmed
extra virgin olive oil, for pan-frying
200 g speck, cut into small dice
18 button mushrooms,
    stems trimmed
12 chat potatoes
50 ml chicken stock
50 g butter
1 bunch flat-leaf parsley,
    leaves picked and chopped

Cut the marylands at the joint to separate the leg from the thigh. Use a knife to trim away any skin from the knuckles. Place the chicken in a bowl and cover with the red wine. Add the carrot, celery, onion, garlic and leek, then cover with plastic film and marinate in the fridge for 24 hours.

Preheat the oven to 150°C.

Drain off the marinating liquid (keep it for later) and remove the chicken and vegetables. Pat the chicken pieces dry with a clean tea towel and season with salt and pepper. Heat a little oil in a frying pan and cook the chicken pieces for 3–4 minutes or until brown on all sides.

Heat the vegetable oil in a large ovenproof saucepan or flameproof casserole dish, add the vegetables and cook over low heat for 5 minutes. Add the marinating liquid and simmer for 10–15 minutes until the liquid has reduced by two-thirds. Add the chicken and enough chicken stock to cover and bring to the boil. Skim the surface, then cover with a lid and cook in the oven for 45 minutes.

Remove from the oven and allow the chicken to cool in the liquid. Using a fine sieve, strain the liquid into a large saucepan and simmer for 10–15 minutes until the liquid has reduced by half. Discard the vegetables. Return the chicken to the reduced liquid and braise until warmed through.

To prepare the garnish, blanch the pickling onions in boiling salted water for 3–4 minutes until tender. Heat a little olive oil in a saucepan and sauté the speck with the pickling onions for 3–4 minutes. Add the mushrooms and sauté for a further 2–3 minutes or until golden.

Cook the chat potatoes in boiling salted water until tender. Allow to cool slightly, then cut in half.

Place the chicken stock and butter in a saucepan and bring to the boil. Add the potatoes, pickling onions, speck and mushrooms to warm through, then stir in the chopped parsley.

To serve, place a chicken leg and a thigh on each plate and spoon the coq au vin garnish over the top.

SERVES 6

Scampi in brik pastry with aïoli and gremolata

A favourite from the ARIA menu, I see this dish as a posh version of fish and chips (with the crisp, golden pastry representing the chips). The pastry is Tunisian brik pastry, which is available from Middle Eastern food stores and good delicatessens. Large king prawns would also work well here if you are unable to find scampi.

12 raw scampi
4 sheets brik pastry
1 egg, beaten
vegetable oil, for deep-frying
12 sprigs celery cress
    or chervil

Gremolata

½ bunch flat-leaf parsley, leaves
    picked and finely chopped
½ clove garlic, finely chopped
50 ml extra virgin olive oil
25 ml lemon juice
salt and pepper

Quick aïoli

100 g mayonnaise
½ clove garlic, crushed
juice of ½ lemon
salt and pepper

To prepare the aïoli, mix together the mayonnaise, garlic and lemon juice and season with salt and pepper. Cover and leave to infuse in the refrigerator for at least an hour, then remove from the fridge and pass through a fine sieve.

For the gremolata, place the parsley, garlic and extra virgin olive oil in a bowl and mix well. Stir in the lemon juice and season to taste with salt and pepper.

Remove the scampi from the shell, leaving only the tail attached. Place the brik pastry sheets in a pasta machine and pass through on the tagliatelle setting. If you don't have a pasta machine, roll up the pastry into a log, cut into 5 mm wide strips, then unroll. Wrap strips of pastry around each of the scampi, brushing a little egg on the ends to help stick them together.

Half-fill a deep-fryer or heavy-based saucepan with oil and heat to 180°C (a cube of bread dropped in the oil should brown in 15 seconds). Add the scampi and cook for about 2 minutes until crisp and golden.

To serve, place the aïoli in the centre of six plates and arrange two pieces of scampi on each. Drizzle some gremolata around the scampi and garnish with a little celery cress or chervil.

SERVES 6

Baked Christmas ham with maple syrup and clove glaze

Every Christmas I bake at least a dozen hams for friends and family. Over the years, these hams have become a culinary collaboration between myself and my brother-in-law Peter, as the glaze is made from his beloved family recipe. The key to success here is to make sure that you evenly cover the ham with the glaze. Use top-quality Canadian maple syrup, which is not too sweet but blends harmoniously with the piquancy of the mustard powder and cider vinegar.

1 leg good-quality ham
30 whole cloves
250 g brown sugar
2 teaspoons mustard powder
60 ml cider vinegar
60 ml maple syrup

Preheat the oven to 180°C.

Remove the skin from the ham, leaving the fat on. Score the fat with a knife in a criss-cross pattern, then place a clove in the centre of each diamond.

Mix together the sugar, mustard powder, vinegar and maple syrup and brush evenly over the ham.

Bake in the oven for about 45 minutes or until heated through and golden brown, basting four or five times during cooking. Remove the ham from the oven and rest for 10 minutes before carving. If you want to make this ahead of time and serve it at room temperature, wrap the cooled ham in plastic film or place in a ham bag and store in the fridge for up to 4 days.

Scallops grilled in their shells with sauce vierge

My favourite scallops are the Tasmanian or king scallops, which have an orange roe and a sweet, rich flavour. Sauce vierge is a simple dressing that also works well with delicate white fish, such as whiting, garfish or fillets of John Dory.

16 scallops on the half shell
salt and pepper
extra virgin olive oil, for drizzling
4 basil leaves, finely shredded

Sauce vierge

2 tomatoes
100 ml extra virgin olive oil
50 ml lemon juice
1 teaspoon coriander seeds,
  crushed

Preheat a grill for about 10 minutes until it reaches its highest heat.

Meanwhile, to make the sauce vierge, blanch the tomatoes in salted boiling water for 10 seconds, then submerge them in iced water for a minute. Remove from the water and peel away the skins. Cut the tomatoes into quarters, then remove the seeds and finely chop the flesh. Combine the olive oil, lemon juice and crushed coriander seeds in a saucepan over low heat and infuse for 4–5 minutes. Stir in the chopped tomato, then remove from the heat.

Arrange the scallops (in their shells) on a baking tray, season with salt and pepper and drizzle with a little olive oil. Place under the grill for 2 minutes – you may need to do this in batches. Transfer the scallops to a plate and spoon the warm sauce vierge over the top. Sprinkle with shredded basil and serve.

SERVES 4

Roast kurobuta pork belly with apple sauce

Who doesn't like pork with apple sauce? Kurobuta pork was originally one of the old English Berkshire breeds but was later developed in Japan (hence the name: kurobuta means black pig). This pork is special because it has fat marbling through the meat, which gives it a luscious flavour and moist texture. A suitable alternative would be Bangalow pork.

2 kg kurobuta pork belly,
   bones removed
300 g table salt
1 teaspoon ground star anise
2 teaspoons white pepper
1 tablespooon ground allspice
1 teaspoon five-spice powder
2 teaspoons fennel seeds, crushed
1 teaspoon ground cinnamon
1 teaspoon ground cardamom
extra virgin olive oil, for rubbing

Apple sauce
300 g castor sugar
100 ml rice wine vinegar
½ vanilla bean, split
5–6 green apples, peeled,
   cored and sliced
juice of ½ lemon

Score the pork with a knife, forming a criss-cross pattern about 1 cm apart. Mix together the salt and spices and rub all over the pork. Cover and leave for 5 hours, then rinse the salt mix off the pork and pat dry with kitchen paper. The pork can now be stored overnight if you wish.

Preheat the oven to 250°C.

Place the pork on a wire rack in a roasting tin, skin-side up, and rub with a little oil. Roast for 30 minutes until the skin is crispy, then reduce the temperature to 160°C. Roast the pork for a further 40 minutes until tender. Remove, cover with foil and leave to rest for 15 minutes.

To prepare the apple sauce, place the sugar, vinegar and vanilla bean in a medium saucepan, bring to the boil and boil for 5 minutes. Add the apples and lemon juice and cook for a further 5 minutes. Remove from the heat and take out the vanilla bean. Transfer to a food processor and blend until smooth.

To serve, cut the pork into slices and spoon the apple sauce over the top.

SERVES 8

Roast confit potatoes
These potatoes are full of flavour and wonderfully crispy. Duck fat is available in tins from specialty food stores.

750 g desiree potatoes,
  peeled and cut into quarters
¼ bunch thyme
4 cloves garlic, unpeeled
1 litre duck fat
salt and pepper

Place the potatoes, thyme and garlic in a saucepan and pour in enough duck fat to cover them. Cook over low heat for 20–30 minutes until the potatoes are soft but not falling apart. Preheat the oven to 180°C. Heat a roasting tin for at least 10 minutes. Drain the potatoes from the duck fat, then carefully pour a couple of tablespoons of fat into the hot roasting tin. Arrange the potatoes in the tin and season with salt and pepper. Increase the oven temperature to 200°C and roast the potatoes for about 40 minutes, turning occasionally, until golden and crispy.

SERVES 6

Mashed potato
To make perfectly creamy, light mashed potato you need potatoes that are floury and dry – such as desiree, sebago or spunta – and lots of elbow grease.

1 kg desiree potatoes, peeled
  and cut into quarters
250 g cultured unsalted butter
500 ml cream
salt and pepper

Place the potatoes in a saucepan of cold salted water, bring to the boil and cook for about 25 minutes or until very tender. Drain. Return the potatoes to the pan and place over low heat for 1–2 minutes to dry out any excess moisture. Using a potato masher, mash the potatoes in the pan, slowly adding the butter and cream. Pass through a fine sieve into a clean saucepan and season to taste. Gently reheat before serving.

SERVES 6

Potato galette
To clarify butter, melt it in a saucepan then let it settle for 3 or 4 minutes. Skim off the foam, then carefully pour the liquid butter into another container, leaving the solids behind.

1.5 kg desiree potatoes,
  peeled and cut into
  1.5 mm thick slices
salt and pepper
500 g clarified butter,
  melted

Preheat the oven to 160°C and line a large baking tray or ovenproof skillet with baking paper. Using a 5 cm circular cutter, cut the potato slices into rounds, then arrange on the baking paper in overlapping circles. Season with salt and pepper and drizzle with the butter. Cover with a sheet of baking paper and place a snug-fitting tray on top. Bake for about 40 minutes until golden brown.

SERVES 6

Barramundi with tomato salsa and fried zucchini flowers

I prefer to use farmed barramundi as it doesn't have the strong earthy flavours that wild-caught barramundi can have. Any leftover salsa will keep for up to 4 days – serve it with spaghetti or potato gnocchi.

40 ml extra virgin olive oil
4 × 160 g barramundi fillets
vegetable oil, for deep-frying
4 zucchini (courgette) flowers
¼ bunch flat-leaf parsley,
    roughly chopped
4 knobs butter
1 lemon

Beer batter
120 g plain flour
50 g cornflour
2 teaspoons baking powder
170 ml beer

Tomato and olive salsa
2 egg tomatoes
2 teaspoons olive oil
1 clove garlic, sliced
5 anchovy fillets,
    roughly chopped
1 tablespoon salted baby
    capers, rinsed
50 g kalamata olives,
    pitted and cut in half

To prepare the beer batter, mix all the ingredients with a spoon until well combined – it doesn't matter if there are a few lumps. The batter can be used straight away or set aside for up to 2 hours.

Preheat the oven to 180°C.

To prepare the tomato and olive salsa, blanch the tomatoes in salted boiling water for 10 seconds, then submerge them in iced water for a minute. Remove from the water and peel away the skins. Cut the tomatoes into quarters and remove the seeds, then cut the flesh into small dice. Heat the olive oil in a saucepan and cook the garlic until it turns translucent. Stir in the anchovies and capers, then add the chopped tomato and mix until all the ingredients are combined. Cover the saucepan with a lid and leave for about 5 minutes, stirring occasionally, until the tomatoes begin to break down. Remove from the heat, add the olives and set aside at room temperature until required.

Heat the extra virgin olive oil in a frying pan. Add the barramundi fillets, skin-side down, and cook for 5–6 minutes until they have caramelised and turned golden brown. Place the barramundi in the oven while you cook the zucchini flowers.

Half-fill a deep-fryer or heavy-based frying pan with vegetable oil and heat to 180°C (a cube of bread dropped in the oil should brown in 15 seconds). Dip the zucchini flowers in the beer batter, then carefully lower into the oil and deep-fry for 4 minutes until crispy. Remove with a slotted spoon and drain on kitchen paper.

Place the salsa in a saucepan to reheat, then stir in the parsley. Remove the fish from the oven, carefully turn it over and place a knob of butter on top (this will soon turn a nut brown colour). Squeeze some lemon juice over the top.

To serve, spoon the tomato salsa onto the middle of four plates and place the barramundi fillets on top. Arrange a zucchini flower on each piece of fish and serve.

SERVES 4

Rib of beef with mustard and parsley

Without doubt, my favourite cut of beef is the aged rib eye (scotch fillet) on the bone. It has a wonderful flavour with just the right amount of fat to keep it juicy. The mustard and parsley form a crunchy crust, so all you need to serve is a few vegetables and a good bottle of red wine.

100 g seeded mustard
½ bunch flat-leaf parsley,
   leaves picked and chopped
2 teaspoons black peppercorns,
   crushed
1 tablespoon sea salt
2.5 kg aged Angus beef rib
Roast confit potatoes (see page
   158), to serve
steamed green beans, to serve

Preheat the oven to 180°C.

Mix together the mustard, parsley, pepper and salt and smear all over the beef rib. Place the meat in a roasting tin and roast for 30–40 minutes, then reduce the heat to 140°C and cook for a further hour. Remove from the oven and leave to rest for 10 minutes.

Carve the rib and arrange the slices on a plate. Serve with roast confit potatoes and steamed green beans.

SERVES 6

something sweet

Buttermilk pancakes with fresh berries My children

Harry and Amelia love pancakes for breakfast, and this is a fail-safe recipe. I usually add a drizzle of raspberry purée with the maple syrup to cut the overall sweetness of the dish, but you don't have to.

3 eggs, separated
2 cups buttermilk
60 g butter, melted
300 g plain flour
1 teaspoon bicarbonate
   of soda
1 punnet strawberries
1 punnet raspberries
1 punnet blueberries
canola oil spray
300 g fresh ricotta
120 ml raspberry purée
   (bought is fine)
maple syrup, to serve

Whisk the egg yolks well, then whisk in the buttermilk and melted butter. Sift the flour and bicarbonate of soda into the egg mixture and fold together.

Cut the strawberries into quarters and mix with the blueberries and raspberries.

Just before cooking the pancakes, whisk the egg whites until soft peaks form and fold gently into the batter.

Lightly spray a heavy-based frying pan with oil and set over medium heat. Ladle in enough batter to form a pancake of your desired size and cook until bubbles form on the top side. Flip over and cook the other side until golden brown. Continue with the remaining batter to make 12 pancakes in all.

To serve, place a pancake on each plate, spoon on some ricotta and scatter with berries. Place another pancake on top, followed by more ricotta and another handful of berries. Drizzle with raspberry purée and maple syrup and serve.

SERVES 6

Espresso parfait

This stylish dessert looks great on the plate and tastes even better! Essentially, it is an ice-cream terrine served with crunchy seed wafers.

Espresso parfait
2 egg yolks
4 tablespoons castor sugar
2 teaspoons coffee extract or
    strong espresso
225 g cream, lightly whipped

Crème parfait
2 egg yolks
4 tablespoons castor sugar
3 teaspoons Baileys Irish Cream
1 vanilla bean, split and
    seeds scraped
225 g cream, lightly whipped

Sesame and
poppy seed wafers
60 g butter
60 g castor sugar
20 ml liquid glucose
20 ml milk
3 tablespoons poppy seeds
6 tablespoons sesame seeds

To prepare the espresso parfait, whisk the egg yolks, sugar and coffee extract until light and pale. Gently fold in the cream, then spoon the mixture into a piping bag. Pipe the mixture into eight 6 cm round moulds until the moulds are half-full, then place in the freezer.

To prepare the crème parfait, whisk the egg yolks, sugar, Baileys Irish Cream and vanilla bean scrapings until light and pale. Gently fold in the cream, then spoon the mixture into a piping bag. Pipe the mixture over the frozen espresso parfaits and return the moulds to the freezer.

Preheat the oven to 180°C and line a large baking tray with baking paper.

To make the sesame and poppy seed wafers, combine the butter, sugar, glucose and milk in a saucepan and bring to the boil. Stir in the poppy and sesame seeds, then remove from the heat and allow to cool. Pour the mixture onto the baking tray (as thinly as possible) and bake for 10 minutes until golden brown. Remove from the oven and cool. Using a 6 cm circular cutter, cut out 16 rounds.

For each serve, place a sesame and poppy-seed wafer on a plate. Place the parfait on top and press gently to remove the mould. Finish with a second wafer and serve immediately.

SERVES 8

Chocolate tart

The success of this tart largely depends on the quality of the chocolate you use. Buy the best you can afford, with a high percentage of cocoa – I like Valrhona or Amedei. Serve the tart with whipped cream or crème fraîche.

520 ml cream
100 g butter, cut into small dice
350 g dark chocolate
100 g milk chocolate
5 eggs
3 egg yolks
cocoa powder, for dusting

Pastry
375 g butter, diced
185 g icing sugar
550 g plain flour
75 g cocoa powder
3 eggs

To prepare the pastry, mix the butter, sugar, flour and cocoa powder in a food processor on low until the mixture resembles breadcrumbs. Add the eggs one at a time and mix until the pastry just starts to come together. Wrap in plastic film and rest in the fridge for 2 hours.

Preheat the oven to 180°C.

Roll out the pastry to a thickness of about 8 mm and ease into a 28 cm tart tin. Gently press the pastry into the tin and trim the edges, then refrigerate until firm. Line the pastry with baking paper and fill with a layer of uncooked rice. Bake for 12 minutes, then remove the paper and rice and bake for a further 8 minutes or until it feels firm when gently pressed. Remove from the oven and set aside to cool. Reduce the temperature to 150°C.

Pour the cream into a large saucepan and bring to a simmer, then remove from the heat. Stir in the butter and both types of chocolate until melted and combined, then add the eggs and egg yolks. Pour the mixture into the tart shell and bake for 15 minutes (it should still have a small wobble in the centre). Remove and cool completely on a wire rack.

Dust with cocoa powder before serving.

SERVES 8–10

Bombe Alaska

The great thing about this dessert is that it can be prepared ahead of time and frozen until needed. Just take it out of the freezer 10 or 15 minutes beforehand and serve with the orange sauce. Pistachio paste is available from delicatessens, some cake shops and large supermarkets. Excess egg whites may be stored in the fridge for a couple of days – use them to make soufflés, pavlovas or an egg-white omelette. You will need an ice-cream machine for this recipe.

Ice-cream
1 litre milk
16 egg yolks
225 g sugar
30 g pistachio paste
250 ml cream

Sponge
4 eggs
125 g castor sugar
100 g plain flour, sifted
20 g butter, melted

Orange sauce
200 g freshly squeezed
   orange juice
25 g sugar

Meringue
7 egg whites
200 g castor sugar

To prepare the ice-cream, bring the milk to the boil in a saucepan, then remove from the heat. In a separate bowl, whisk the egg yolks, sugar and pistachio paste, then pour in a little of the warmed milk. Stir together, then pour the egg mixture into the milk and cook over low heat, stirring constantly, until the mixture coats the back of a spoon. Strain the liquid into a bowl set over iced water, stir in the cream and pour into an ice-cream machine. Churn according to the manufacturer's instructions.

For the sponge, preheat the oven to 190°C and line a baking tray with baking paper. Using an electric mixer, whisk the eggs and sugar until they are pale, then fold in the flour and then the butter. Pour the mixture into the baking tray and bake for about 8 minutes or until golden. Remove from the oven and allow to cool on a wire rack. Using a 3 cm circular cutter, cut out eight rounds.

To prepare the orange sauce, combine the orange juice and sugar in a saucepan and simmer until the liquid has reduced by three-quarters.

To prepare the meringue, place the egg whites and castor sugar in an electric mixer and whisk at high speed until the mixture has the texture of shaving cream.

Scoop the ice-cream into balls the size of a golf ball and place on top of the sponge rounds. Coat the ice-cream and sponge with the meringue mixture, then using a kitchen blowtorch, cook the outside of the meringue until it is golden. If you don't have a blowtorch, you can cook the meringue in a very hot oven for about 1 minute.

Serve immediately with the orange sauce.

SERVES 8

Poached strawberries with moscato granita

This simple dessert is best made in summer when there is an abundance of fresh, ripe strawberries. The moscato granita has a delicate flavour and smells of roses and lychees – it could also be served with poached peaches or pears.

250 g sugar
50 ml strawberry liqueur
2 punnets strawberries, hulled
finely grated zest of 1 lemon

Moscato granita
100 g sugar
juice of 3 lemons
350 ml moscato

To prepare the moscato granita, combine the sugar and 375 ml water in a saucepan, bring to simmer, then immediately remove from the heat. Stir in the lemon juice and moscato, then transfer the mixture to a shallow container and place in the freezer. While the mixture is freezing, rake with a fork occasionally to form crystals.

To poach the strawberries, combine the sugar, strawberry liqueur and 250 ml water in a saucepan and bring to a simmer. Add the strawberries then remove the pan from the heat. Place a small piece of plastic film over the strawberries to ensure that they remain submerged in the liquid and gently poach until tender. Leave the strawberries to cool in the liquid.

Cut the strawberries into quarters and place in a bowl. Add the lemon zest and toss gently, then divide the strawberries among eight glasses or small bowls. Spoon the moscato granita over the top just before serving.

SERVES 8

Peanut and praline ice-cream in brandy-snap baskets

If you are making these delicate biscuits in summer, don't prepare them too far in advance as humidity will soften them quite quickly. The brandy-snap mixture could also be rolled into a cylinder and filled with ice-cream, flavoured cream or mousse. You will need an ice-cream machine to make the peanut and praline ice-cream.

500 ml milk
6 egg yolks
100 g castor sugar
300 g cream

Brandy-snap baskets
120 g butter
140 g brown sugar
180 ml liquid glucose
2 teaspoons brandy
140 g plain flour

Peanut praline
100 g sugar
200 g salted peanuts,
    roasted

To prepare the brandy-snap baskets, process the butter and brown sugar in a food processor for 3 minutes until light and fluffy. Add the glucose and brandy and process until incorporated. Transfer the mixture to a bowl and carefully fold in the flour. Cover and refrigerate for an hour.

Preheat the oven to 160°C and line a baking tray with baking paper.

Using a tablespoon, scoop out eight portions of the brandy-snap mixture. Roll each portion into a ball with your hands, then flatten to a disc about 10 cm in diameter. Place the discs on the baking tray and bake for 8 minutes until golden brown. Remove from the oven and cool for 30 seconds. Working quickly, carefully peel each disc from the tray and place it on an upside-down mug, pressing the sides down to form a basket. Set aside to cool and set, then store in an airtight container until required.

To make the peanut praline, line a baking dish with baking paper. Place the sugar and 50 ml water in a saucepan, bring to the boil and cook until the mixture becomes a light-golden caramel. Add the peanuts and stir to coat with the caramel, then remove from the heat. Pour the mixture into the baking dish and set aside to cool for 30 minutes or so. When cool, roughly chop the praline.

Bring the milk to the boil in a saucepan, then remove from the heat. In a separate bowl, whisk the egg yolks and sugar until light and thick. Pour the milk into the egg mixture, then return the mixture to the saucepan and place over low heat. Cook gently until the mixture coats the back of a spoon, stirring constantly, then strain into a bowl set over a bowl of iced water. Allow to cool, then stir in the cream and pour the mixture into an ice-cream machine. Churn according to the manufacturer's instructions. When the ice-cream has thickened, stir in three-quarters of the peanut praline, then place in the freezer.

To serve, place a brandy-snap basket in the centre of each plate. Scoop balls of the ice-cream into each basket, scatter with the remaining peanut praline and serve immediately.

SERVES 8

Trifle

I like to serve this modern version of trifle in late summer, usually after a light seafood meal. Serve it in individual glasses so you can appreciate the layers.

6 gelatine leaves, softened
   in cold water
4 eggs
125 g castor sugar
100 g plain flour, sifted
20 g butter, softened

Poached stone fruits
750 ml champagne
320 g castor sugar
3 white nectarines
3 peaches
6 plums

Custard
4 egg yolks
100 g castor sugar
½ vanilla bean, split
   and seeds scraped
500 ml double cream
500 ml cream
1 gelatine leaf, softened
   in cold water

To prepare the poached stone fruits, combine the champagne, sugar and 350 ml water in a large saucepan and bring to a simmer. Submerge the nectarines and peaches in the liquid and simmer gently for about 10 minutes until they are tender. Remove the fruit. When cool enough to handle, peel the fruit and cut into wedges. Bring the liquid back to a simmer and add the plums, then turn off the heat and set aside for 5 minutes or until tender. Remove the plums and reserve 400 ml of the poaching syrup for the jelly. When the plums are cool, peel them and cut into wedges.

To make the jelly, heat the reserved poaching syrup and 100 ml water in a saucepan. Squeeze any residual water from the gelatine leaves and stir into the poaching liquid. Pour into a small container and place in the fridge for an hour or so to set.

To prepare the custard, place the egg yolks, sugar and vanilla bean scrapings in a bowl and whisk the ingredients together. Combine the creams in a saucepan and gently heat. Stir some of the hot cream into the egg yolk mixture, then pour the mixture into the remaining cream and cook over low heat, stirring constantly, until the liquid coats the back of a spoon. Stir in the softened gelatine, then strain. Pour into an airtight container and store in the fridge until required.

Preheat the oven to 180°C and line a 20 cm cake tin with baking paper.

Using an electric mixer, whisk the eggs and sugar until they are pale, then fold in the flour and then the butter. Pour the mixture into the tin and bake for about 12 minutes until cooked (a skewer inserted into the centre should come out clean). Remove from the oven and cool in the tin for a few minutes before transferring to a wire rack to cool completely. Cut the cooled sponge into 2 cm cubes.

Place a piece of peach, nectarine and plum in each serving glass, then add a layer of sponge cake. Place a spoonful of custard on the cake, followed by a spoonful of jelly. Repeat the layers until the glasses are full, then store in the fridge until required. Garnish with any remaining fruit just before serving.

SERVES 6

Grilled apricots and sauternes sabayon

When I was growing up on our family farm at Badgerys Creek, we had a huge apricot tree in the front garden. Back then, I spent more time throwing them at my brother than eating them, but these days I love to cook with them. The sabayon is a real treat and makes a wonderful foil for the apricots, but it can also be served with strawberries or blueberries with some amaretti biscuits crumbled over the top.

35 ml dessert wine (sauternes)
3 egg yolks
200 g castor sugar
100 ml thickened cream,
   lightly whipped
6 apricots
6 slices brioche, toasted
10 amaretti biscuits, crushed
2 punnets raspberries

To prepare the sabayon, place the wine, egg yolks and half the castor sugar in a bowl set over a saucepan of boiling water and whisk for 8–10 minutes until it becomes thick and holds its shape. Pour the mixture into a bowl and whisk until it cools down and becomes thick and creamy. Gently fold in the thickened cream, then place the mixture in the fridge.

Cut the apricots in half and coat the cut side with a little castor sugar. Place them on a baking tray, cut-side up, and cook under a hot grill for about 4 minutes or until tender. Carefully turn the apricots over, sprinkle with the remaining sugar and grill until they are lightly caramelised.

Cut the brioche slices in half and remove the crusts, then cut into rectangles.

To serve, spoon the sabayon into shallow bowls and top with the brioche. Arrange the grilled apricots on the brioche and finish with crushed amaretti biscuits and raspberries.

SERVES 6

Profiteroles with vanilla ice-cream and caramel

The key to making good profiteroles is to make sure that each pastry ball is cooked through and dry in the middle. The best way to test them is simply to pick one up – if it feels light and crisp, it's cooked. You can fill them with whipped cream if you like, but I prefer vanilla ice-cream – it's perfect with the caramel sauce.

125 ml milk
110 g butter
1 teaspoon castor sugar
½ teaspoon salt
140 g plain flour, sifted
5 eggs

Caramel
200 g sugar
200 g butter
200 ml cream

Vanilla ice-cream
500 ml milk
1 vanilla bean, split
8 egg yolks
110 g sugar
125 ml cream

To prepare the caramel, heat the sugar and 50 ml water in a saucepan over high heat, stirring constantly until it begins to caramelise. Brush the sides of the saucepan as required to prevent the sugar crystallising. When the mixture becomes a dark caramel colour, carefully stir in the butter followed by the cream. Boil for 1 minute, then remove from the heat and allow to cool.

To prepare the vanilla ice-cream, gently heat the milk and vanilla bean in a saucepan. When hot, cover with a lid and leave to infuse for 1 hour. In a bowl, whisk together the egg yolks and sugar, then carefully stir in a little of the infused milk. Pour the egg yolk mixture into the milk and cook over low heat, stirring constantly, until the mixture coats the back of a spoon. Strain the liquid into a bowl set over iced water, stir in the cream and pour into an ice-cream machine. Churn according to the manufacturer's instructions.

To prepare the profiteroles, preheat the oven to 200°C and line a baking tray with baking paper. Bring the milk, butter, castor sugar, salt and 125 ml water to the boil in a saucepan, then stir in the flour. Cook the dough, stirring constantly, until it starts to come away from the sides of the pan. Transfer the dough to an electric mixer. Using the paddle beaters, beat until the dough is lukewarm, then add the eggs one by one and mix until combined. Set aside to cool.

Place generous tablespoons of the dough on the baking tray, leaving plenty of room for spreading as they will triple in size when cooked. Bake for 15 minutes, then reduce the temperature to 150°C and cook for a further 8–10 minutes until dry.

To serve, cut the profiteroles in half and place a scoop of vanilla ice-cream in each bottom half. Replace the lid of each profiterole. Drizzle with caramel and serve.

SERVES 6–8

Beer-battered banana fritters

This dish is a childhood favourite of mine, and is a quick and easy dessert for winter. I like to serve it with chocolate ice-cream and roasted pecans.

250 ml beer
20 g fresh yeast or
    10 g dried yeast
180 g plain flour, sifted
vegetable oil, for deep-frying
4 ripe bananas
castor sugar, to serve

Combine the beer and yeast in a small saucepan and warm gently until it reaches blood temperature (that is, neither hot nor cold to touch). Slowly stir in the flour until combined, then leave to prove for about 30 minutes or until bubbles begin to form on top.

Half-fill a heavy-based frying pan or deep-fryer with oil and heat to 180°C (a cube of bread dropped in the oil will brown in 15 seconds).

Cut the bananas into 3 cm logs and coat them in the beer batter, allowing the excess batter to drain. Carefully lower the bananas into the oil and cook for about 4 minutes until they become golden and crispy. Remove the bananas from the oil and drain on kitchen paper. Toss them in some castor sugar and serve immediately.

SERVES 4

Poires belle Helene

I have a sentimental attachment to this dish because I completed my four-year apprenticeship at a restaurant called 'La Belle Helene' in Sydney. This classic French dessert can be served with vanilla or caramel ice-cream, or try it with warm custard that has been flavoured with pear liqueur.

6 Beurre Bosc pears
750 ml champagne or
    dessert wine (sauternes)
300 g castor sugar
1 vanilla bean, split
vanilla ice-cream, to serve

Chocolate sauce
60 g cocoa powder
120 g castor sugar
25 g butter

To prepare the chocolate sauce, place the cocoa, sugar and 200 ml water in a saucepan and bring to the boil, stirring constantly. Boil for 2 minutes, stirring, then whisk in the butter. Remove from the heat and allow to cool.

Peel each pear, carefully remove the core from the base (using a small melon baller or the pointed end of the peeler) and trim the base so it sits flat. Combine the champagne, sugar, vanilla bean and 250 ml water in a large saucepan and bring to a simmer. Add the pears, then cover the pan with baking paper and simmer for 20 minutes until the pears are cooked through. Check with a wooden skewer – it will slide in and out easily if the pears are cooked. Leave to cool in the syrup.

To serve, divide the pears among six bowls and add a scoop of vanilla ice-cream. Pour the syrup and chocolate sauce into separate jugs and serve on the side.

SERVES 6

Bread and butter pudding

When I make bread and butter pudding I prefer to use fruit bread rather than white bread, as it adds both flavour and texture. Serve it piping hot with vanilla ice-cream and a glass of dessert wine.

1 loaf sourdough fruit bread
5 eggs
4 egg yolks
125 g sugar
small pinch nutmeg
½ vanilla bean, split and
    seeds scraped
450 ml milk
450 ml cream
15 g butter, melted

Cut the fruit bread into 1 cm thick slices and leave uncovered on the bench for a few hours to become stale (this helps the bread to absorb more custard).

Preheat the oven to 160°C.

Place the eggs, egg yolks, sugar, nutmeg and vanilla bean scrapings in a bowl and gently stir with a whisk until combined (try not to incorporate too much air as you stir).

Gently heat the milk and cream in a large saucepan, add the egg mixture and stir to combine.

Lightly brush the bread slices with the melted butter, then arrange them in a large ovenproof dish, making sure the slices overlap. Carefully pour the custard over the top. Gently push any bread slices that have floated up back into the custard. Set aside for 15 minutes to allow the bread to soak up the custard.

Place the dish in a roasting tin and half-fill the tin with water to create a water bath. Bake for 35 minutes. To check whether the pudding is cooked, shake the dish gently – the centre should have just a slight wobble. Cook for a further 5–10 minutes if necessary. Remove the pudding from the oven and place under the grill to brown a little, if required.

SERVES 8–10

Chocolate mousse

Chocolate mousse seems to be a favourite dessert for kids and adults alike. Here, it is topped with hazelnuts, though you could also top it with orange segments and crumbled honeycomb, or perhaps some fresh summer berries.

450 g dark chocolate
  (no more than 55% cocoa)
1 litre thickened cream
4 egg yolks
100 g hazelnuts, roasted
  and chopped
whipped cream, to serve

Melt the chocolate in a very dry bowl set over boiling water – make sure you don't let any water come into contact with the chocolate. Once melted, remove from the heat and set aside for about 3 minutes to cool slightly.

In another bowl, whisk the thickened cream until soft peaks form.

Whisk the egg yolks into the melted chocolate, then whisk in half of the cream until well combined. Using a large metal spoon, carefully fold in the remaining cream, working quickly to retain the airy texture. Pour the mousse into eight individual bowls or cups and place in the fridge for about 3 hours or until set. You can make this a day in advance if you like.

Just before serving, scatter the top of the mousse with chopped hazelnuts and serve with a bowl of freshly whipped cream.

SERVES 8

Custard-apple cheesecake

Custard apples are an unusual fruit with a rich, sweet flavour that seems to combine strawberry, mango and notes of pineapple in one mouthful! Always discard the black seeds before using the creamy white flesh. I love to make this cheesecake for afternoon tea and serve it with some caramelised apples . . . yum!

375 g Granita (wheatmeal) biscuits
375 g Ginger Nut biscuits
450 g butter, melted
4 large or 6 small custard
  apples, peeled and seeded
100 g sugar
juice of 2 lemons
750 g cream cheese, at room
  temperature
6 eggs
200 g sour cream

Sour cream topping
250 g sour cream
juice of 1 lemon
25 g icing sugar, sifted

Preheat the oven to 160°C. Line a 22 cm springform tin with baking paper.

Crush the biscuits in a food processor until they are the consistency of fine crumbs, add the melted butter and mix until combined. Press the biscuit mixture into the tin while it is still warm, then place in the fridge until the biscuit base hardens.

Purée the custard apple and pass through a sieve. Place in a food processor, then gradually add the sugar and lemon juice, pulsing to combine. Add the cream cheese a little at a time, followed by the eggs and sour cream, processing until combined. Pour the mixture into the tin over the biscuit base and bake for 50 minutes.

To prepare the sour cream topping, mix together the sour cream, lemon juice and icing sugar until combined.

Check the cheesecake to see if it is cooked by gently shaking the tin (the cake should only wobble slightly in the centre). Remove the cheesecake from the oven and smooth the sour cream topping over the top. Return to the oven and bake for about 5 minutes.

Remove the cheesecake from the oven and cool to room temperature, then refrigerate to cool completely before serving.

SERVES 8

Christmas pudding with brandy custard

Every year at the restaurant we make about 200 puddings to give to our regular customers. Christmas pudding really improves with age – the longer it keeps, the more complex the flavour becomes. If you like, top it up with a few nips of brandy every few months to keep it moist and fortified. It may seem a little strange to use beef suet in a sweet dish, but it really does make a difference to the flavour and texture of the pudding. If you prefer, you can replace the suet with vegetable shortening, which can be found in supermarkets.

180 g dried figs, chopped
130 g seedless raisins
50 g dried apricots, chopped
75 g mixed peel
90 g brown sugar
180 g beef suet, grated
100 g plain flour
90 g dried breadcrumbs
grated zest and juice of 1 orange
grated zest and juice of 1 lemon
1 vanilla bean, split and seeds
    scraped
1 nutmeg, grated
2 eggs
75 ml brandy
600 ml milk
butter, for greasing

Brandy custard
500 ml thickened cream
½ vanilla bean, split
8 egg yolks
100 g castor sugar
35 g cornflour
35 ml brandy, or to taste

To prepare the pudding, mix together all the ingredients in a large bowl, then cover with plastic film and refrigerate overnight.

Grease a large pudding bowl with butter and spoon in the pudding mixture. Wrap the bowl tightly with several layers of plastic film to make it waterproof. Put the pudding bowl in a large saucepan, then fill the pan with water until it is 2 cm from the top of the bowl. Cover the pan with foil, bring the water to the boil and boil for about 4 hours, replenishing the water every 40 minutes or so. Check to see that the pudding is cooked – a wooden skewer inserted into the centre should come out clean. Remove the bowl from the saucepan and cool to room temperature.

Remove the wrapping from the pudding, seal with a new layer of plastic film and store in the fridge. When ready to serve, rewrap the pudding as above and reheat it in a large saucepan of boiling water for about 30 minutes.

Meanwhile, prepare the brandy custard. Pour the cream into a medium saucepan, add the vanilla bean and bring to the boil. Whisk together the egg yolks, sugar and cornflour in a bowl. Stir a small amount of the cream into the egg yolk mixture, then gradually pour the mixture into the remaining cream and cook gently for about 10 minutes until thickened, stirring constantly. Strain the mixture through a fine sieve and set aside to cool. Add the desired amount of brandy just before serving with the pudding.

SERVES 8–10

Coconut macaroons

These coconut-flavoured biscuits are great with tea or coffee, or serve them as a petit four after dinner.

220 g castor sugar
85 g desiccated coconut
55 g shredded coconut
30 g plain flour
6 egg whites
20 chocolate buttons

Preheat the oven to 180°C and line a baking tray with baking paper.

Combine the sugar, desiccated and shredded coconut and flour in a bowl, then transfer to a saucepan. Add the egg whites and stir until well combined. Place the saucepan over medium heat and stir for 10–15 minutes until the mixture starts to come away from the sides. Remove from the heat and allow to cool.

Shape the mixture into 20 balls. Place a chocolate button on top of each one and push it into gently into the ball. Transfer to the baking tray and bake for 5 minutes until golden. Cool on a wire rack before serving.

MAKES 20

Lemon and lime tart

A good lemon and lime tart should have a smooth, glossy curd, a fresh, tangy flavour and a crisp pastry base – and it should always be eaten on the day it is made. There are many different recipes around, but I swear by this one. When making the pastry, use your fingertips to rub the butter into the flour as this is the coldest part of your hand and will stop the butter getting too soft.

4 eggs
3 egg yolks
300 g castor sugar
300 ml lemon juice
75 ml lime juice
225 ml orange juice
450 ml thickened cream

Pastry
300 g plain flour
90 g icing sugar
180 g butter, cut into 1 cm dice
1 egg, lightly beaten

To prepare the pastry, combine the flour and icing sugar, then rub in the butter until the mixture resembles breadcrumbs. Add the egg and mix gently until a dough forms. Cover with plastic film and rest in the fridge for 2 hours.

Preheat the oven to 180°C.

Roll out the pastry to a thickness of about 8 mm and ease into a 27 cm tart tin. Gently press the pastry into the tin and trim the edges. Line the pastry with baking paper and fill with a layer of uncooked rice. Bake for 15 minutes, then remove the paper and rice and bake for a further 5 minutes until golden. Remove from the oven and set aside to cool. Reduce the temperature to 150°C.

In a bowl, mix together the eggs, egg yolks and sugar, then stir in the juices and cream. Transfer to a saucepan and stir over a low heat until hot to the touch. Strain the liquid through a sieve into a jug.

Place the tart shell on a baking tray. Pour half the filling into the tart and transfer it to the oven (if you fill it to the top you are likely to spill some). Pour in the remaining filling mixture. Bake for 15 minutes, then rotate the tin to ensure even cooking and bake for a further 10 minutes. Jiggle the tart carefully – there should be a small wobble in the centre. If the whole tart wobbles, bake for a further 5 minutes. Serve with cream.

SERVES 8–10

Champagne jelly

This delicate dessert could also be served with summer fruit, such as mangoes, nectarines or white peaches, to offset the sharp acidic flavour of the jelly.

8 gelatine leaves
500 ml champagne
100 g castor sugar
mixed berries, to serve
small mint leaves, to garnish

Place the gelatine leaves, champagne and 400 ml cold water in a medium saucepan over low heat until the gelatine dissolves. Add the castor sugar and stir until it dissolves. Skim away the debris and then pour the jelly into six serving glasses. Refrigerate overnight to set.

When ready to serve, spoon some mixed berries over the jelly and garnish with mint leaves.

Another way to make this is to pour half the liquefied jelly into the glasses and allow to partially set, then place the berries on top and fill the glass with the remaining jelly. Refrigerate overnight to set.

SERVES 6

Churros with chocolate sauce

Churros are Spanish doughnuts that are piped in a long star-shaped log and served with a chocolate dipping sauce. Make sure the oil is at the correct temperature – if it is not hot enough, the churros will absorb the oil and taste greasy, and if it is too hot, they will overcook. To maintain the oil temperature, you must resist the temptation to cook too many at once.

125 ml milk
125 g butter
60 g castor sugar
½ teaspoon salt
150 g plain flour, sifted
3 eggs, lightly beaten
200 g dark chocolate
    (preferably 64–70% cocoa)
vegetable oil, for deep-frying
30 g castor sugar, extra

Combine the milk, butter, sugar, salt and 125 ml water in a heavy-based saucepan, bring to the boil, then remove from the heat. Stir in the flour with a wooden spoon. Set the pan over medium heat and stir until the mixture comes away from the sides of the pan and has a grainy texture. Remove the pan from the heat, pour the mixture into a bowl and leave to cool for 5 minutes. Gradually add the beaten egg, stirring until well incorporated and the dough starts to come together in a ball. Cover with plastic film and chill in the fridge for a couple of hours until firm.

To make the chocolate sauce, simply melt the chocolate in a bowl over a saucepan of just-simmering water (don't let the bowl touch the water). This should only take 5 minutes. Keep in a warm place while you make the churros.

Half-fill a large, heavy-based saucepan with vegetable oil and heat to 180°C (a cube of bread dropped in the oil should brown in 15 seconds).

Place the dough in a piping bag that has a star tube inside. Carefully pipe the dough straight into the hot oil, cutting it into lengths with a pair of scissors. Cook for about 5 minutes or until the churros are golden brown in colour, turning with a slotted spoon so they cook evenly. Remove and drain on kitchen paper. Repeat with the remaining dough.

Sprinkle the extra sugar over the churros and serve hot with the pot of melted chocolate for dipping.

MAKES 20

acknowledgements

Thanks to all the wonderful staff at ARIA for giving me time to work on other projects, and in particular:

My head chef, Ben Turner, who not only looked after the restaurant but also helped with the recipes. My pastry chef, Andy Honeysett, and Laura Baratto, for helping me with the shooting of the book.

The girls in the office – Megan Lowe, for endlessly typing and retyping recipes, and Karen Evans, for telling me where I should be every hour of the day.

My business partners, Peter and Susan Sullivan.

My beautiful family, Sarah, Harry and Amelia.

At Penguin, Julie Gibbs, Adam Laszczuk, Alison Cowan, Rachel Carter and Megan Baker – plus brilliant photographer Alan Benson and stylist Yael Grinham.

A special note of love and gratitude to the most amazing maître d and beautiful friend, Peter Bartlett. He will be sorely missed.

index

We would like to thank Sunbeam Australia (sunbeam.com.au) for generously providing a barbecue for recipe testing and photography, and Stylecraft (stylecraft.com.au) for the Hoopla Sled dining chairs used in the photo shoot.

LANTERN

Published by the Penguin Group
Penguin Group (Australia)
250 Camberwell Road, Camberwell, Victoria 3124, Australia
(a division of Pearson Australia Group Pty Ltd)
Penguin Group (USA) Inc.
375 Hudson Street, New York, New York 10014, USA
Penguin Group (Canada)
90 Eglinton Avenue East, Suite 700, Toronto ON M4P 2Y3, Canada
(a division of Pearson Penguin Canada Inc.)
Penguin Books Ltd
80 Strand, London WC2R 0RL, England
Penguin Ireland
25 St Stephen's Green, Dublin 2, Ireland
(a division of Penguin Books Ltd)
Penguin Books India Pvt Ltd
11 Community Centre, Panchsheel Park, New Delhi – 110 017, India
Penguin Group (NZ)
Cnr Airborne and Rosedale Roads, Albany, Auckland, New Zealand
(a division of Pearson New Zealand Ltd)
Penguin Books (South Africa) (Pty) Ltd
24 Sturdee Avenue, Rosebank, Johannesburg 2196, South Africa

Penguin Books Ltd, Registered Offices: 80 Strand, London WC2R 0RL, England

First published by Penguin Group (Australia), a division of Pearson Australia Group Pty Ltd, 2009

10 9 8 7 6 5 4 3 2 1

Text copyright © Matthew Moran 2009
Photographs copyright © Alan Benson 2009

The moral right of the author has been asserted

All rights reserved. Without limiting the rights under copyright reserved above, no part of this publication may be reproduced, stored in or introduced into a retrieval system, or transmitted, in any form or by any means (electronic, mechanical, photocopying, recording or otherwise), without the prior written permission of both the copyright owner and the above publisher of this book.

Designed by Adam Laszczuk © Penguin Group (Australia)
Styling by Yael Grinham
Typeset in 9.5/14pt Fonce Sans Pro by Post Pre-press Group, Brisbane, Queensland
Colour reproduction by Splitting Image, Clayton, Victoria
Printed and bound in China by 1010 Printing International Ltd

National Library of Australia
Cataloguing-in-Publication data:

Moran, Matt.

When I get home / Matt Moran;
with photography by Alan Benson.

9781921382055 (hbk.)

Includes index.
Cookery.
Benson, Alan.

641.5

penguin.com.au

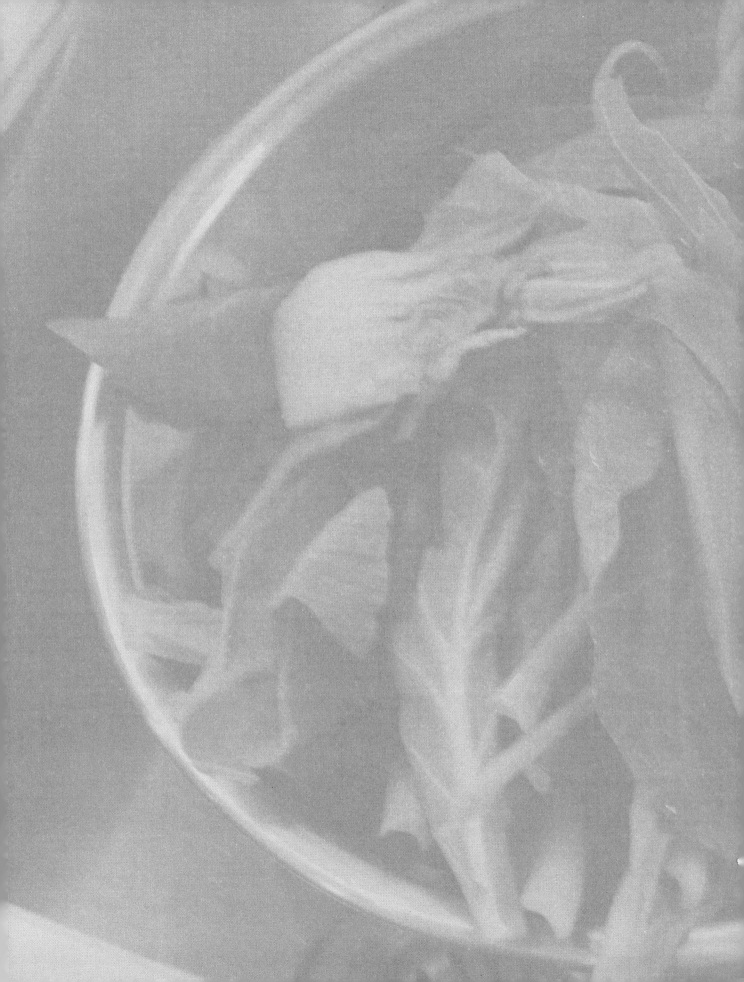